Rough Design

Salvatore Bommarito
July 11 2011

ISBN: 1466290897
ISBN-13: 9781466290891
Library of Congress Control Number: 2011916104
CreateSpace, North Charleston, SC

Chapter 1

"You better keep your goddamn mouth shut."

"Don't threaten me, and don't try to frighten me." She knew the man on the phone was a very dangerous person. He was desperate and worried about having problems with the law.

"I swear to God, I'll burn your fucking business to the ground and kill you and your family if you talk to the cops."

"I'm not talking to anybody, Jake."

"Listen to me carefully, Ms. Best," his voice was dripping with sarcasm. "You're up to your gorgeous ass in this scam. You've been cheating your clients for years. I know. I have all the records to prove it. Don't go soft on me now. We've made a lot of money together. Haven't we?"

"Yes. I'm not going to jeopardize our moneymaking arrangement. I've worked too hard, so relax. We need to extricate ourselves from the current problem. So, don't harass me, just fix it."

"I'll take care of it."

Best said, "Let's change the subject. I have a new client with a huge order, maybe two and a half million."

"Sounds great. Tell me more."

"Just take care of the unhappy guy first."

"Will do."

Alexandra Best hung up the phone and adjusted her short Armani skirt. It rode up her thighs during the heated conversation. She never installed a modesty shield on the front of her desk. Viscerally, she understood the advantages of showing leg while conducting business. It excited the men and made the women uneasy; this was a good thing as the men were usually the ones paying her invoices.

Maybe, she was in too deep and needed to reconsider the Gordon deal, as well as future "collaborations" with Jake; perhaps she was being too greedy. A fleeting thought, but then Best did the arithmetic: 400 thousand dollars on top of a two million order. No way was she cutting down this money tree.

Of course, there was still the unhappy client who was accusing Best of gouging him. She was confident that Jake would deal with Gordon. After all, this was his specialty. She decorates homes, screws clients between the sheets, as well as between the lines of their invoices, and he and his goons intimidate uncooperative clients. A simple quid pro quo arrangement, but it worked.

Alex smiled as she was ruminating. Life isn't all that difficult to understand, she thought. It boiled down to a very simple, easily applied algorithm: screw or be screwed. Why do people insist on making it so complicated?

She stood up, grabbed her Prada bag and admired herself in one of the many mirrors in her elaborate office suite. Pleased with what she saw, she knew what she had to do and was absolutely certain that she had the assets, some natural others surgically enhanced, to do it. Alex was at the top of her game.

Chapter 2

My name's Stoke Spencer, and my firm is Pyglet, an investment bank. My colleagues and I help companies merge together; and we arrange complex financing transactions. Banking is a cutthroat field in which I have distinguished myself in scores of transactions over the years.

For a long time, the Street took notice of my success, and Pyglet's reputation grew exponentially. Without sounding terribly self-serving, my personal reputation regarding my business acumen has become legendary. My exploits, commercially and carnally, have reached mythical proportions. Bullshit! In all honesty, the former has far exceeded the latter.

But, time takes a toll on hard-working bankers, and a lot of time has passed. My business achievements have begun to ebb along with my drive and ambition, although I continue to enjoy very significant compensation and a windfall of residual benefits. Luckily, the financial crisis didn't have a substantive impact on my business.

Usually, I play the role of senior advisor in the firm's transactions, but I've empowered Rob Viand, a brilliant long time colleague and stud extraordinaire, to close my deals. I just love the guy, however, I'm more than a little envious of his incredible physical gifts, self-confidence and animal magnetism. He's currently attached and married to another colleague who has been the subject of so many of my prurient thoughts.

"Will you please pick up your freaking phone, Stoke? It's that crazy broad calling for the third time today."

My longtime assistant, Liz, has become accustomed to speaking to me in this manner; it's my fault. I've allowed it, and at an unconscious level, encouraged it. It feels like being with one of the guys. It's not unusual for Liz to curse me out, make sexual innuendos and explicitly reference male and female body parts in her verbal interactions with me. I love it! Liz shoots straight from the hip; I never have to read between the lines. She's also incredibly competent at doing that which I pay her handsomely to do. One of her many tasks is screening all of my calls, personal and business.

When I first hired Liz (almost two decades ago), I was somewhat uncomfortable and, indeed, reticent to make her cognizant of my more intimate relationships. However, I quickly learned that in order for her to do that which I absolutely needed her to do, she had to be aware of my darker side.

"Just tell her I'm busy."

"No. You've been ravaging the poor woman. The least you can do is speak with her."

"Since when are you responsible for the mental health of my girlfriends?"

"Stoke, you're a pig. You know it, and everyone knows it. You're a male whore."

"Liz, stop exaggerating. I only have sex with women who are willing. I don't ravage females unless they want to be ravaged. Have I ever come on to you or made you feel uncomfortable?"

"No offense, you wouldn't survive a night with me, boss," she said sarcastically with a smirk on her face. Actually, Liz Palmer has said that to me many times during the time she's been my assistant. If she wasn't a big haired, five foot eleven, 175-pound Amazon from the mean streets of Queens, I might take her for a ride.

On second thought, she might cripple me in the throes of passion with her thunder thighs. Now that's a scary thought.

"Okay, okay. Shut my door. This might get rough." My partners and associates in the office have heard this type of banter frequently as I navigate through multiple relationships with some very unsavory and mentally challenged women. The worst of which is my ex-wife, SS, officially known as Sharon Spencer. I wish the bitch would change her name, so I'd no longer be associated with her. "Hello. How are you Darla?" Darla Johnson.

"Stoke, why aren't you returning my calls?"

"I'm busy, sweetheart."

"You don't treat me like your sweetheart."

"Whatta ya mean? You're a doll. I'm crazy about you." Darla is a 40-something year old former model, who might have barely made it past sixth grade. She doesn't work anymore because her third husband paid her a fortune to take a hike. Along the way, Darla learned that it's profitable to retain a good attorney when she has a domestic quarrel with a boyfriend or husband.

And, she's really great to look at. What the hell, she spends half of every day in the gym and eats rabbit food. Moreover, she's an extraordinary piece of ass. But when Darla speaks, you never know what the hell is going to come out of her mouth.

"Stoke, you only want to see me when you're horny. You never take me out with your friends. Do I embarrass you?"

I would never ask Darla to a social event. She's too dumb although all the men would lust after her voluptuous body. Plus, Darla dresses like a slut, which is not a bad thing. She intimidates other women. She's so attractive, but alas, she's a birdbrain. "You don't embarrass me. I'd just rather be with you alone. When we go out with others, I have to listen to the same old crap, the economy, Barack Obama and all that. When I'm with you, we can focus on making each other happy."

"You want me for my body, not my mind."

Ding, ding, ding! That's absolutely correct. When you wrap those long legs around me, it's like heaven. When you start screaming, I'm on top of the world. "Don't say that, honey. I love to hear your opinions on everything." Especially political issues. What a joke.

"I've been very depressed since I saw you on Saturday night. My life's a mess. I don't ever do anything intellectual. I just work out and have sex with men."

So what's wrong with that? That's why you're so good in bed. Practice makes perfect. "Darla, you have a great life. And, your not sleeping around on me, are you? I'd never do that to you." Of course I would and am doing so regularly.

"I feel like killing myself."

"Please Darla, don't talk crazy. You have too much to live for." There are still hundreds of men who should have an opportunity to slip off your thong.

"I mean it, Stoke. What you do to me is what every man does. Wham bam, thank you ma'am."

Why is it so difficult for this woman to recognize her true calling in life? She fornicates like a prostitute and isn't too bright except when it comes to domestic settlements. "Come on, you're just having a bad day. Do you want me to come over?"

"Why, so you can get your rocks off?"

Well yes. Naturally. "I want to make you feel better."

"Okay. How about one?"

"See you then."

As I hung up the phone, Rob knocked on my door and walked into my office. "When your door's shut, you're usually having a conversation with a bimbo. Am I right?"

"You got me. That's why I like you so much. You're so deductive. Darla is threatening to commit suicide, so I have to go over to her place to talk her out of it. I'll do it while we're humping." I started to laugh. I really amuse myself sometimes.

"We have lunch today at 12 with the CEO of W Pictures. The company wants to do some kind of big deal. I need you at the meeting."

"Well, you got me for a half an hour. Then, I must do my duty. What's W Pictures' business?"

"They make soft core pornographic films."

"Should we be involved with porno companies? Will we get to meet some of their female stars?" I immediately had mixed feelings.

"That would be a side benefit of helping the company."

"Okay, so have your meeting."

"Why do I do all the work around here, and you make all the money?"

"That's bullshit. You made $8 million last year. What the hell do you want?"

"$10 million, which is what you paid yourself."

"I deserve it. I founded Pyglet, and you're nothing but a glorified office boy."

"Don't insult me, Stoke."

"If you're so damn smart, why do you need me at your meeting?"

"I don't. But, I'd never commit to anything without your approval, you'd bust my balls eternally if I did."

"Right. So behave yourself."

"Seriously, I think this guy wants to borrow a ton of money, pay himself a dividend and cash out a large part of his investment in the company."

"Don't sweat it. I'll be there, and I'll be charming as usual."

"I don't want this to go to your head, Stoke, but every client wants to meet you and hear what you have to say. The great Stoke Spencer, investment banking guru."

"That's a good thing; and don't forget it."

"They should only know that while you have a great financial mind, you're such a loser with women. They might also find it somewhat amusing that you date hookers."

"Are you suggesting that Darla performs sexual acts for money? She's loaded. She doesn't have to use her body to pay her bills."

"She still looks and acts like a slut."

"I like that. Get out of here and make me some money. By the way, how's married life", I asked with a grin on my face.

"Great. Why don't you go to Laura's desk and ask her how we are doing?" He walked out. I didn't know how to interpret his remark. Laura and I "almost" had a fling a few years ago before she and Rob got married. I was just about to hit pay dirt in the middle of the night in my office when Liz staggered in after a night on the town and caught us with our pants down. She was furious. To make a long story short, Laura lawyered-up and sued me for sexual harassment, but after I helped her with a serious problem, she forgave me. Rob and Laura then rekindled their relationship and eventually got hitched. He used to be an incredible lady's man, so I've always been skeptical about his desire to be monogamous for the rest of his life. Maybe, he's having issues with his wife.

Laura is so beautiful. We call her "The Thong." Since she's been married to Rob, she stopped wearing tight white pants that enabled us to see the outline of her thongs, and her skirts are now longer covering up her creamy white thighs. I wish I had finished our business that night. She's always been my sexual fantasy.

Chapter 3

Upon graduation from Yale's School of Art, Goldfarb shipped out to La La Land to begin his career with the whackos and perverts in the West Coast film industry. He became known as one of the more creative young filmmakers in town, although he knew immediately that he would never get rich working with big-time directors and famous movie stars.

But, there were many perks to working in the movie business. And, Goldfarb never missed an opportunity to hit on young and aspiring actresses. It was like shooting fish in a barrel especially with his good looks. Everybody was screwing everybody in those days. You had to be wary of ending up in bed with a person of the same sex while in your daily drug or alcohol-induced stupor.

Eventually, Goldfarb's escapades caught up with him. A court-appointed psychologist labeled him a sex addict after he was accused and convicted of sexual harassment by a group of starlets. They formed a cabal, hired a scumbag ambulance chaser and filed a class action suit against him and his employer. The plaintiffs said the company created a hostile environment for women. All it meant was that the guys wanted to sleep with the actresses, which was absolutely true. Goldfarb didn't have any money so his employer paid the babes a few thousand apiece to put a stop to the litigation.

The mandatory therapy group he was ordered to attend wasn't so bad. He met women who were sex addicts and equally interested in sexual pursuits as he. "Sex addict" is a really stupid term if you think about it. By definition, it's likely that over 75% of all single men under 30 years of age are, by definition, sex addicts. At one point, Goldfarb was accused of abusing "helpless" women in his group. Really, he was just having consensual sex with several of them in his car after class.

The lead psychologist of his therapy group, a flaming lesbian who despised all heterosexual men, reported him to the judge who originally assigned Goldfarb to her. The shrink was pissed Alan was scoring with the hot babes in class, and she wasn't.

"Mr. Goldfarb, what's wrong with you?" The judge asked him.

Donning his most contrite look, Alan answered, "Sorry, your honor, I don't know what you mean."

"Are you completely incapable of controlling your sexual appetite? Is there no limit to your cravings? Why must you torment every woman you meet?"

"I really enjoy being with women, and most women enjoy being with me. Ms. Crotch, the psychologist, doesn't like me very much so she said I was misbehaving." There was some giggling in the courtroom.

"Her name is Koch, not Crotch." The judge corrected Goldfarb.

Koch yelled out, "The man's a pig, your honor."

"Calm down, Ms. Koch."

"I apologize, your honor," Goldfarb said grinning.

"Mr. Goldfarb, you just can't have sex with every female in Hollywood. Some don't appreciate your advances."

"Aw, judge, you're kidding with me, right?"

"Son, I'm not making a joke. You're getting on my nerves. I bailed you out of a serious situation a while back, but you've been unable to rein yourself in. Continuing to sexually harass women has brought you back to my court."

"I had consensual sex with every single one of them, your honor."

"That's not what they said. Even the female sex addicts in your group think you're a predator."

"I'm sorry your honor. I guess I have a strong libido."

"Well, now you're going to pay the price. I'm putting you in the city jail for 30 days. No women in there so you'll just have to manage."

"Please judge, give me one more chance."

"Nope. You're in for 30 days. I suggest you leave LA after you do your time. If I see you in my court again, you're going to do hard time."

Goldfarb went to jail and somehow avoided any intimate moments with his male roommates. After being released, he decided it would be wise to get out of town to avoid any further confrontations with the judge. Where should he go? Well, New York City has a thriving film industry and plenty of available babes. He loaded up his modest belongings in his 1975 Dodge Dart and headed east.

Goldfarb found work easily as his experiences were in great demand at the time. Again, he wasn't getting rich but made a good living. And, the chicks were plentiful and just as easy as the ones on the West Coast.

After a few years, he decided to set out on his own. Goldfarb set up shop in Manhattan in an empty loft and became a big hit filming soft-core pornography, the kind that's televised on cable after 11 p.m. He was tempted to make more explicit films, but thought, once you make those kinds of movies, there was no turning back. And so, he chose the name W Pictures, which is one letter away from X (rated).

During his life, Goldfarb had more sex than 99% of the males on the planet. Being over six feet tall, very athletic and having the good looks of a movie star made it easy for him to recruit actresses for his movies. All young girls want to become actresses. Many of them are ready, willing and able to do nudes scenes, but few would agree to graphic sex in front of a camera. So, Goldfarb filmed them having simulated sex and then had real sex with them himself after the filming ended.

Goldfarb married three different women; the first two relationships ended quickly. He just couldn't keep zipped up. When he turned 55, he met his current wife, Denise, who was an aspiring 25 year-old actress. She's beautiful and intelligent having graduated from Syracuse University with a degree in Psychology. Maybe, that's what Goldfarb needs, a live-in shrink. Nevertheless, being married again didn't stop him from seducing the women he hired for his movies. Denise, at first, was disturbed by his inability to be loyal, but soon got over it and became sexually active herself around town. She preferred young and energetic men, who were less experienced and very aggressive in bed. It was an unholy alliance, but Goldfarb needed a regular escort, and Denise needed his money, so they coexisted.

The Goldfarbs live in a 15-room townhouse located on the Upper East Side. He continues to spend long hours at work while Denise shops and works out.

Recently, Goldfarb decided to purchase a home in the Hamptons. He wanted to slow down a bit as he approached his 60th birthday. Maybe he'd take up golf and start to work out regularly. In any case, he purchased a large house on the water in Bridgehampton. It was in mint condition but needed to be redecorated.

Chapter 4

Damien Spencer, my older son, graduated from college two years ago. He wasn't the best student in high school because he really didn't work very hard. His mother and I were in the process of divorcing, and, I'm sure, our fighting and screaming attributed to his bad attitude. But, I have to give SS credit (and I don't do this very often) for getting Damien to finish high school, apply to college and actually gain admittance.

Being away at Boston University was a good thing for my son. Actually, being away from all the bullshit at home enabled Damien to get his life together. The good news is that he posted very good grades and didn't mess with drugs, although, I suspect he drank more than his fair share of alcohol.

Damien's real passion was sex, a chip off the old block, except he's really good looking. His six foot two inch frame, an athletic build he honed at the gym and a sharp tongue resulted in numerous encounters during his four-year stay in Boston.

There was one scare that needed my attention, in which Damien allegedly impregnated a coed. The kids are so promiscuous that it's often difficult to ascertain who the daddy is without a DNA test. In any case, SS told me about the problem, and I did what any upstanding wealthy father would do, I bribed the girl to shut up and paid for an abortion. Damien didn't need to plead to anything. I just made the problem go away with cash.

I had a man-to-man talk with him about using technology that combats pregnancies and disease (commonly known as a condom). He dutifully listened, but I'm sure my sage counsel went in one ear and out the other. I suppose I wasn't a very good role model for him. He should only know how I choose my sexual partners.

I reflected on my conversation with him afterwards and had very mixed feelings. On the one hand, I believed women deserved to be treated with respect and intimacies should be based upon some kind of deep feelings. But, I never lived up to this ideal. Rather, sexual gratification was the be all and end all for me. Frankly, I don't give a shit about anybody's feelings when I'm horny. So, I did feel like a hypocrite as I pontificated to my son. But, you know the old saying, don't as I do, do as I say.

After graduation, we had a family meeting, SS, Damien, my other son, Jason, and me. The topic was what should Damien do with his life moving forward. I thought I might avoid a similar confrontation with Jason in the future if he sat in on this discussion. We bandied about possibilities such as law school, travelling abroad for a year, working at Pyglet (Damien, immediately trashed the idea of working with me) and the film industry.

Damien took a number of film courses in his senior year while he majored in psychology. I guess he wanted to study psychology to try to figure out why his parents were so screwed up. Anyway, he lost interest in his major along the way but managed to do well academically. The woman who he "might" have impregnated was a film student and turned him on to the subject.

The conversation was not very productive as Damien had already made up his mind. I told him that the odds of getting a job in the film industry were slim, and the possibility of earning a living was even slimmer. Although he pretended to listen, I was just blowing a lot of hot air as far as Damien was concerned. And so, he began to seek employment in the film business.

A few months passed and Damien asked SS and me to meet with him a few days ago. He had news about a job and wanted to discuss it with us. I couldn't understand why he gave a shit about our opinions, but maybe, something good was about to happen. We met at SS's apartment, the one I pay for every month. Jason was out getting into trouble and was not present.

I walked into SS's building located on Park Avenue and greeted the doorman.

"How are you, Joe?"

"Fine, Mr. Spencer, how you doin'? Haven't seen you in a while."

"Would you come here willingly to see my wife?"

"I understand your point." He tried to hide his smile. Basically, he was stipulating that SS was a total bitch, who treated every service person like they were a piece of garbage.

"Will you buzz Mrs. Spencer, please? She's expecting me so she will probably say it's okay for me to go up." I smiled.

"No problem. We miss seeing you, sir."

I always gave the staff large bonuses during the holidays and treated them with respect. It's nice to be appreciated. "Thanks, but I don't miss living here." I walked towards the elevator bank.

When I arrived at SS's floor, I knocked on the door and walked in. Nobody locks his or her door on Park Avenue, especially if there's only one apartment on the floor. I looked around and apparently SS had been busy redecorating. New Oriental rugs, new window treatments, new furniture adorned the place. Wow. I must have spent a ton on this stuff.

"Hi Stoke."

"Sharon."

"Damien's in his room getting dressed. He'll be out in a moment."

"You've done a lot of work here. I must be paying you too much alimony."

"The apartment needed a few things. And, don't try to bait me. What's your problem anyway?"

"Sharon, my monthly checks to you are insanely high. I shouldn't be responsible for redecorating your Park Avenue home. We should talk about a reduction."

"Tell your attorney to call mine if you have a gripe."

"You're looking fit for an old broad. Are you still working out with that muscle bound ape of a trainer?"

"I'm not an old broad. But thanks for the left handed compliment anyway. Yes, Juan is still my trainer."

"The Latin lover, huh?"

"Does that turn you on? Frankly, he could care less about me. He only wants my money, and besides, he's gay. You're such a good judge of people, ha."

"You mean my money. You don't have any of your own."

"It always comes back to cash flow with you, doesn't it? Let me spell it out for you. You married me, and then we divorced. You earned all the money while I stayed home raising your kids. In New York, that entitles me to one half of the pot. It's a simple formula."

"You really are looking great. Maybe I made a mistake giving up your hot body."

"You're full of shit. You walked out. It's your loss."

"The problem was you weren't in good shape when we were together, and I can't remember ever kissing those beautiful breasts, much less any other parts of your body."

"You're a pig. Are you trying to seduce me? You have such a way with words. I think you've been watching too many dirty movies."

"To tell you the truth, I would take a tumble with you if you promised not to talk. You could scream and beg for more, but nothing else."

"Well, that's never going to happen. You'd have to accept the mouth and the vagina as package deal."

"Now that's a great line. If I ever write a book about our relationship, I'll be sure to use it and give you credit. I would substitute another word for vagina, though." I started to laugh.

18

"Pig."

Sharon was really decked out for our meeting. She was wearing an Anne Fountaine sleeveless white top. I could see her pert nipples through the sheer blouse and bra. The top complimented her Prada skirt that extended below her knees over tanned legs and Manolo four-inch heels. Her hair is much longer and straightened. It fell down past her shoulders. Too bad, she had to use a fair amount of makeup to hide the crow's feet around her eyes. For an upper forty-something year old woman, she looked damn good.

"Well, look what the cat dragged in," Damien said to me. Nice way for a kid to greet his father.

"If you're trying to welcome me, you're getting off to a lousy start."

"I hope you two lovebirds are getting along. Is there a reconciliation in the works?"

"Damien, I hate your mother, and she feels the same way about me. Don't get your hopes up."

"Well, I really don't care anyway."

I started to get hot under the collar. I'm used to taking grief from SS, but Damien was another story. "What the hell am I doing here? My ex wife can't stand me, and my son treats me like shit. Let's get this meeting over with quickly. I have things to do."

Damien glared at me. "Nothing's change, has it? You always have something else to do."

"Not a goddamn thing, son."

"Fair enough. I thought I should tell you two that I found a job and will be getting my own place in the Village."

Damien looked amazing. He was buff with long dirty blonde hair, designer jeans that were intentionally ripped at the knees and a long-sleeved black shirt.

"Congratulations. What's the name of your employer, what does the company do, and what are you going to do for the company?" My due diligence begun.

"It's a film company you never heard of. I'm going to be an assistant director for new movies."

"Sounds great. What kind of movies does the company make?"

"Soft porn."

"Terrific," I said. "You're going to work in the pornography business?"

"Yup. And pornography is a bigger industry than you think."

"Really. How big is it?"

"Ten billion each and every year. Everybody watches porn, young and old. It helps old men like you get aroused."

"I don't need any assistance, thank you."

SS said, "You're not going to perform in any of these movies, are you?"

"Not sure at this point. My boss needs me to expedite the filming process. Time is money, you know. But, if I like a script, I might jump in."

"Porn flicks don't have scripts. All the actors and actresses do is grunt, scream and cry." I responded.

"Whatever."

I had had enough, "Are you out of your mind. The business is chock full of scumbags and venereal disease. These movie producers prey upon young girls and seduce them into participating in degrading acts, which you are now going to film."

"Dad, you don't know what you're talking about. Scores of beautiful women are breaking down the doors trying to become actresses. If they need to fuck to get a job, they do it."

"No kidding," I said sarcastically. "Actually, I had an experience with a woman named Cleopatra, an African American porn star."

SS was mortified by this revelation, "Stoke, what is wrong with you. You date porn actresses. Do you see hookers as well?"

"Let me finish. She got mixed up with some nasty characters and was murdered. There's a lot of really dangerous people associated with the business."

"I hear what you're saying, Dad. My boss is a good guy, who runs a legitimate shop. Nobody is forced to do anything he or she is uncomfortable with. Actually, the female stars pick the male actors they want to work with, and the sex acts they are willing to do."

"Why would you ever agree to be in a porn movie?"

"It could be a stepping stone to a more traditional acting career. I've got an appointment, so I'm out of here. Mom, I'll be moving out next week. You guys have fun together."

SS and I stood in the foyer, where all this took place, and stared at each other. We never even sat down.

She said, "I'm speechless."

I responded, "I need a drink."

"I'll join you. It's after five."

We knocked off a bottle of red and chatted for an hour about Damien's new career. I had a feeling I was about to enter the danger zone with this woman, whom I truly despise.

"Why don't you relax, Stoke? Take off your jacket and shoes. I'll put on some music."

"I should be running along."

"Oh, stay a while. We have so much more to talk about."

"Damien is making a mistake. Porn is an awful business that will never be legitimate, no matter how hard the producers try to justify it."

"I always fantasized about acting in a porno movie."

"Please, Sharon. You could never be in a dirty movie. You're too disgusted by sex."

"Not true, Stoke. I've been completely liberated by some of the men I've dated since we split up."

"Really. And did you engage in any advanced sexual activities?" Sharon was skulking around the room having already shed the Manolos. After hiking up her skirt to mid thigh, she sat down across from me giving me an unobstructed view. "Well, yes I did."

Why was I encouraging this? "You're a liar. During our marriage, you'd only have sex in the missionary position. You mean to tell me that now you're swinging from the rafters? I don't believe it."

"Well, now I like to be had in many different positions."

"TMI. Why are we discussing this? The last time you seduced me, Damien walked in on us. And, I never even finished."

"Well, I did get off. Too bad you had to leave unsatisfied. My recollection is that that was the first time we ever had sex where you didn't ejaculate in less than a minute."

"You seem to be satisfied at the time, shaking and screaming for more."

"It was really good, Stoke." She started to approach me and sat down at my side. Our open mouths came together forcefully, and I tasted blood.

"I think I'm bleeding, Sharon. My lip is bleeding. You smashed into me so hard, you drew blood."

"Don't worry about it." She grabbed my crotch and started to unzip my pants.

I reacted as she grabbed my testicles and squeezed. "What are you doing?"

"I'm trying to turn you on, stupid."

"It feels like your trying to castrate me." I pulled away, attempted to zip up and accidentally caught my penis in my fly. I gave out a muffled yelp, and Sharon backed off.

"What's wrong with you? Don't you like women anymore?"

"You're despicable. I never could figure how you were going to react to me in any given situation especially if it was sexual. When we lived together you acted like you hated me every time I touched you. Now, you've become too aggressive, you've cut my penis and gave me a fat lip.

"Fuck you, Stoke. You just can't seem to get it right with me. You don't know what you're missing."

"Yes, I do. And, I'm glad I am." I walked out and continued to work on my zipper. Fortunately, I was able to prevent serious damage to my private parts.

Chapter 5

Best Design is one of the top interior decorating companies in the New York Metropolitan area. Alexandra Best founded it ten years ago after she interned for several renowned decorators in the city. All of her former bosses knew she was going to be a smash in the business. Not only is she intelligent, she's beautiful, creative and extremely ambitious. And, she'd do anything to win a piece of business.

New York City experienced two boom periods during the past few years during which Best cleaned up financially. The investment bankers were making a fortune, and their wives couldn't wait to spend hundreds of thousands, and even millions, of dollars, to tear down and renovate coop apartments in New York and huge houses in the Hamptons. After the physical space was refurbished, Alex did her magic and transformed 3,000 to 25,000 square feet into virtual palaces.

Best's style and in your face attitude sometimes was disquieting for the ladies of the house. But, the men loved her. And since the men usually had the power of the purse, money was never an issue. After it was all over, just about every wife loved Alex's work even when many of their mates were smitten by her charm and raw sexuality.

The truth be told, Alex's flirtations with her clients occasionally ended in the bedroom. In some cases, Best and her male clients had a drink and perhaps dinner. But a number of them got to enjoy some of Alex's more exotic skills. These trysts never evolved into full-fledge affairs. Alex just wanted to close deals and, from time to time, have some steamy sex with rich and powerful men. None of the men were looking for long-term relationships either, and they were more than happy to take a tumble with her after they hired Best Design.

Best Design had ten employees including Alex. The ability of the company to grow was limited because Alex had to originate and close every deal. She could never teach another person to be a commercial animal of her stature. Because of this, Alex was resigned to the fact that her business could never be a billion dollar enterprise. After all, not everyone could be Martha Stewart.

In response to this epiphany, Alex started to be more creative in the way she billed her clients and defrauded them regularly with the help of her go-to furniture supplier in North Carolina, Carolina Furniture Company. Basically, she would receive invoices from Carolina that were jacked up 30-40% and pass bogus costs on to her customers. She would then split the loot with her partner down South.

On this day, Alex decided to dress more conservatively because she was recruiting a new designer, Amanda Lane, an up and coming young star in the business. Amanda is beautiful but understated even though she was nearly six feet tall. Alex thought she should dress down a tad for the meeting, at which she hoped to seal a deal with the woman. Usually, Alex was not shy about exposing a lot of breast or leg or both to men or women. Today, she chose leggings, a long blouse and three inch Jimmy Choos.

"Alex, Ms. Lane is in the reception area."

"Bring her to my office."

The receptionist knocked on her door and announced Amanda's arrival. Alex came from behind her glass pedestal desk and greeted the woman warmly. "How are you my dear?"

"I'm just fine, Alex."

Best evaluated her choice of clothing for the meeting. After all, her sense of style would go a long way towards making her successful in the business. Amanda wore all black, black slacks that showed off her figure and a tight black sweater that hugged her beautiful upper torso. Flats de-emphasized her height while a long stand of small pearls was a perfect counterpoint to her ensemble noir. "You look terrific. I take it you spend quite a bit of time at the gym." Actually, Best thought she looked delicious. From time to time, Alex would bed down women, but favored men because of that one special piece of equipment. For a deal, however, Best would be happy to go down on a trophy wife and/or her husband.

"I've been pretty busy, so I don't work out as much as I should."

"Well, have you made a decision about coming to work at Best?"

"Yes, I think Best would be a wonderful place for me. I've been here several times and met most of your colleagues. They're all very nice. And, a chance to learn from Alexandra Best would be dream come true." Actually, Amanda had second thoughts about accepting an offer from Alex. The reasons generally had to do with Alex's lifestyle and reputation. She had heard rumors that her new boss was not shy about mixing business with pleasure. Amanda had an active social life, but would never use her sexuality to win business. Nevertheless, the opportunity and the money were very good so she decided to take a chance that Alex's personal habits would not be too much for her to bear.

"Great. Can you start tomorrow?"

"I don't see why not. I already told my current employer that I was leaving this week."

"Then it's a deal." All the financial considerations had already been discussed and negotiated.

"Perfect." Amanda left walking on air.

Best felt a little tingly when she thought about Amanda. Usually women didn't affect her in this way, but Amanda really was a knockout, attractive, classy and a lot of woman. Best concluded that she needed to stifle the sexual urgings flashing through her mind and body. Sex would come later if Amanda fit in.

More important, Best wanted to use Amanda for the Goldfarb assignment. She thought back to her original conversation with Alan. She could tell he was one of the ubiquitous rich and aggressive types she met so often. What the hell, he was in the porn business. Alex felt she should be offended by his occupation, but his money was as good as anyone else's.

Goldfarb indicated to her that a friend recommended her with one reservation. His friend, and Best's current client Tom Gordon, thought that Best Design had overcharged him. Gordon said Best's work was amazing but something seemed fishy about her invoices.

In fact, Gordon's situation had become much more contentious since Goldfarb spoke with Gordon. Best's last conversation with Tom was a screaming match during which Gordon threatened to speak with the authorities.

For whatever reason, Gordon never told Goldfarb about the latest confrontation. Maybe that was because Best and Gordon had sex in every room of the house she was decorating for him one afternoon a few weeks ago. In fact, Best was the first woman to have sex in the new round bed that Gordon bought for his wife. She considered whether Gordon told Goldfarb about the free, uninhibited sex that could be part of an overall deal with her. She laughed to herself and thought it paid to advertise.

Best was scheduled to meet Goldfarb the next day at W Pictures. It should be interesting. Maybe he'll give her a tour of a porn movie set. In spite of this, Alex decided to bring Amanda along and wondered whether she would be willing to do "anything" to land a deal.

Chapter 6

I met with Rob and Alan Goldfarb from W Pictures for about 20 minutes. Naturally, I had a deep interest in W's business because Damien was about to get into the smut industry, and it involved beautiful, naked women. Alan told us that he wanted to sell the company or do a recapitalization and take out a lot of money; either type of deal would be great for Pyglet. The transaction size would likely be several hundred million dollars that would go directly into Goldfarb's pocket.

After about 30 minutes, I excused myself indicating that I had another appointment. The actual reason for my early departure was that I had a date with a voluptuous nymph for an afternoon of heavenly pleasure, a nooner, as it's referred to. The client was more than a little perturbed that I had to leave as he correctly surmised I was the real decision maker at Pyglet. He struck me as the kind of person who wouldn't put up with attitude, but we shall see. He wanted us to help him take money out of the company, so he'd have to deal with my quirky behavior. I told Rob to schedule another meeting so I could learn more about W Pictures and perhaps watch some actresses having fake orgasms.

It was sunny outside, late spring, and all the crazies were on the street during lunch hour. There was a panhandler on every corner. Why don't these people get a job? It seems to me that begging was much less profitable and more stressful than digging ditches and making a guaranteed wage. But, I guess these characters were either mentally ill, or they were entrepreneurs who couldn't work for other people.

Personally, I'm a sucker for destitute women. I almost always drop a dollar in their paper cup as I pass. The guys are another thing altogether. If they appear to be sane and able-bodied, I ignore them. If they look really down and out, I might give them a tip.

The entire homeless situation in New York City is beginning to really grate on me. Why the hell can't we get these people off the streets, feed them, clean them and train them?

Some homeless dude was sitting on the sidewalk near the subway entrance harassing every person for money, especially the women. A young gal passed too close to him, and he grabbed her leg. I decided to come to the damsel's rescue.

"Take your filthy hands of her, you cad." Actually, I didn't call him a cad. He wouldn't know what the hell I was talking about.

He answered in no uncertain terms, in a way that I was clear about his intentions. He said, "Fuck you, man. Mind your own goddamn business."

I kicked his arm freeing the hysterical woman. By now, she was screaming bloody murder. "Relax honey, I'll take care of this guy." Pretty brave, huh?

The bum tried to get up, and I knocked him down to the ground. He was a big guy, but drunk, so I didn't think he was much of a threat. "Stay down, or I'll keep kicking you."

Then I heard some fellow say, "Leave him alone, tough guy."

I turned around and a young man was towering over me. "Listen pal, I'm just trying to help the lady. I'm a good guy."

"You think you're some kind of hero kicking a drunk man lying on the ground?"

"No, I don't. I just saved that hysterical woman over there. What's your problem?"

He shoved me. "You're my problem, asshole. That man has enough to deal with without jerks like you harassing him."

I tried to shove him back, and he redirected my lunge sending me onto the ground. "You better keep your hands off me, or I'll have you arrested." I said. The bum re-entered the struggle by spitting at me.

"If the police show up, I'll have them arrest you for assaulting that poor guy." He pointed at the bum.

I got off the ground, wiped the spit off my face and shirt, which left a brown stain and walked away. This goddamn city is really starting to get on my nerves. No good deed goes unpunished. There are bums all over the place groping innocent women. I step in to save one of them and get thrown around by a gorilla. My shirt was a mess and my pants were ripped. One $2,500 Zegna suit down the crapper.

Finally, I arrived at Darla's place on 64th street near First Avenue. The building was post war, maybe 30 years old, in pretty good condition. Uniformed men, who kept the riffraff from entering, manned the lobby. You had to be announced to get to the elevators. I suspected the doormen have seen a number of men schlepping up to Darla's place to get a piece of ass.

"Should I ring up Ms. Johnson?" He smiled at me. The guy obviously recognized me as one of the studs who visited Darla from time to time.

"Yeah. I'd appreciate it."

"What happened to you? Did you get mugged?"

"I got into a little scuffle with Tarzan, wasn't anything."

"You okay."

"I'm fine, but I had to beat the shit out of the other guy," I lied.

"Too bad you ripped your suit."

"Had to protect myself. That's the way it goes." He should only know the real story.

"You can go right up."

Darla was waiting by her door. She was dressed for action, no bra, thong and nothing else. I guess she knew what I had in mind.

She was amazing. I stared at her boobs, and they stared back at me. "Come in, honey. You look terrible."

"Well, you look fantastic." I wondered whether Darla really understood what I wanted from her. Did she really think we could have a long-term, substantive relationship?

"Thanks. What happened?"

"I got into a tussle with a tough guy. I saved a woman, who was being accosted by a homeless guy, and some jerk started a fight with me." I emphasized me. "I had to teach him a lesson and put him down." I figured I might as well stick with the story I gave to the doorman.

"Why'd he do that?"

"Good question. I should have cleaned out his wallet to pay for my suit. Come here and make me feel better." I hugged her and her large breasts pushed against me. Our tongues did a tango together as I caressed both cheeks of her ass that flared out from the thong. She smelled great, like a French whore right out of the shower. But for some reason, I wasn't responding properly.

Darla could sense that I was upset and something was wrong. "Just forget about that idiot who attacked you. Think about me and what I'm going to do with you."

"I am, and that's the problem."

"What?"

"I'm not getting aroused."

"Oh that's nothing. It happens from time to time. I'll fix it in no time."

"Let me tell you something, Darla. When I see a woman like you, and she's naked, I'm usually at full mast immediately."

"That's so cute. You mean like a flag pole, right?"

"Right. Well, it's not happening."

"Sit down and relax. I'll work on you, and it'll be fine."

Darla undressed me and did a number of her best moves on me. She rubbed every important part of her body against me, and then kissed all of my sensitive spots. Nothing. I was petrified. This never happened before. Suddenly, someone started pounding on the door.

"Open the fucking door," he screamed. Darla looked petrified.

"Who the hell is that?" I asked.

"It's one of my boyfriends. He's crazy."

"How did he get past the doorman?"

"When you see him, you'll know. You better get dressed."

"Darla, let me in," he bellowed again.

"Okay, Nicky. Give me one second. Stoke, you better put something on before I let him in."

"I'm dressing as fast as I can." In my haste, I caught my penis in the zipper again and yelped. My member seems to be getting in the way a little too often.

"Darla, is someone in there with you?"

"I'm coming. Faster, Stoke."

I cringed from the abrasion but managed to have my pants and shirt on by the time Darla opened the door. Darla was in her original state, mostly nude.

"Who's the chump?" Nicky was about 6-3, and 230 pounds and looked like a linebacker.

"This is Stoke. He's a friend of mine. Stoke, this is Nicky Ollansky. He plays football for the Miami Dolphins."

Great, he was a linebacker. I'm about to get another beat down, from a professional football player.

"Hey Nicky. I was just leaving."

"Maybe you should get out of here before I fuck you up."

I put my coat on and scooted out the door. "Bye Darla."

"Bye, Stoke. Call me sometime."

As I left, I heard Nicky reading the riot act to Darla about seeing other men. I didn't want to hear anymore and streaked towards the elevator. On the way out, the doorman tried to apologize, but I walked right past him feeling lucky that the monster didn't rip me to shreds.

Chapter 7

The next morning, Alex prepared for her meeting with Alan Gold-farb. She put together a collection of photographs of previous jobs on her conference room table that she wanted to show her prospective client.

Her portfolio was quite impressive as she decorated scores of homes in the Hamptons over the years. Because Goldfarb's home was in Bridgehampton, one of the most exclusive and expensive areas on the eastern tip of Long Island, Alex limited the photographs to large homes in beach communities.

While Alex was in the throes of putting together her presentation, Amanda knocked on her door and walked in. "Good morning, Alex."

"Same to you." It was a few minutes before 8 a.m. "You're here nice and early. I like that. You get brownie points on your first day." Both chuckled at Alex's comment.

The fashion contest between the two women had now officially begun. Yet, the contrast between them was striking. Best was wearing a short skirt that was at least three inches above her knees. Amanda was puzzled how she could work comfortably being so exposed especially when she sat down. It being late Spring, the material was cotton with a beach print. After all, the house to be decorated was near the ocean. Her top was white linen, under which she wore no bra. Later a linen coat would cover her torso.

Amanda was embarrassed when she noticed, and envied, how firm Alex's breasts were. She wondered whether they were redone by one of the plastic surgeons in the City. Her shoes were expensive flats, something that surprised Amanda. She thought Alex's long and tanned legs would be beautifully accentuated with heels. In any case, Amanda thought she looked sensational. "You look great. I love your skirt. It's so apropos."

"That's the theme, isn't it? We're going to do some beach-like decorating on Goldfarb's mansion." Alex noted Amanda's couture. She wore a skirt that reached mid calf. It was tapered and adorned with birds on a turquoise background. Amanda's long legs and great figure made the skirt very sensual. Her cotton top was loose fitting, and she donned a white coat over it. Three-inch heels gave the woman a statuesque look. Alex felt a hormonal surge as she examined her assistant's choice of clothes and her willowy body. She wondered how she would look nude on silk sheets with her long hair splayed out on a pillow. "You look sensational, yourself. I hope our clothes will be appropriate for Goldfarb's business environment."

"You mean because all the other women will be naked." They both laughed. Amanda googled Goldfarb last night and got a sense of what type of movies he produced. She was no prude, but this visit promised to be very interesting and somewhat disquieting.

"Maybe Goldfarb will ask us to undress before we make our presentation." Alex winked at her associate.

"Well, we need to use every club in the bag to be successful in this competitive business. But, stripping for a client would take the concept to new level."

"I'm sure the experience won't be too bad. But, you're right about using all your assets." She smiled and returned to the photographs.

At noon, armed with a twenty picture portfolio of completed jobs, the two women hopped into a taxi and headed to W Pictures, which was located on the west side of Manhattan. As they climbed into the taxi, the driver, a young man with an unpronounceable European name, smiled. He turned around and watched Best and Amanda climb in the car hoping to see some leg.

Alex noticed his wandering eyes. "What the fuck are you looking at?"

"Seldom do I have such handsome women in my taxi."

"Handsome?" Best replied. "Don't you know that handsome is a way to describe men, not women, in this country. Why don't you just turn around and drive."

"Yes, madam. I'm sorry to make you uncomfortable. I was admiring your beautifulness."

"Look, we have some business to discuss. Concentrate on getting us to our destination in one piece."

"Okay. Okay. You American women are very aggressive."

Alex decided to ignore the driver's comment but said to Amanda not to quietly, "Goddamn sleaze balls are all over the place."

"Come on Alex, don't let this guy upset you."

"You're right. I'm sorry I lost my temper. It seems like every time I walk down the street, every man I pass is undressing me."

"It's the price you pay for being beautiful."

Best said, "You're sweet," as she fondled her colleague's bare knee. Amanda found the gesture a bit intimate but let it slide.

When they arrived at the W Picture's building, they noted that it was a nondescript two-story structure, more like a warehouse than a movie studio. Alex pressed a button near the door. She spotted a camera overhead. There was a buzz, and they entered a small anteroom. Suddenly, a very attractive dark-haired young woman in extremely tight jeans and a shirt that ended well above her waist appeared. "Are you Ms. Best?"

"Yes, and this is my associate Amanda Lane."

"Please come with me." They were lead down a hallway covered with posters of movies made by W Pictures. Neither woman recognized any of the titles, and each picture featured seductive and mostly naked women.

Alex whispered to Amanda, "Have you seen any of these films?"

Amanda pretended to be thinking about the question and responded, "I don't think so." They laughed out loud. Their escort turned around and smiled knowing that they were making a joke about the posters.

Finally, they entered an area with expensive furniture and a few high-end offices. A receptionist then led them to Goldfarb's spacious quarters.

"Well hello," He said with delight. "Now, I know why Tom Gordon enjoyed working with you so much. Alex Best, I presume." He shook Best's hand firmly but gently at the same time. Then, looking at Amanda, "And you are?"

"Amanda Lane. It's nice to meet you Mr. Goldfarb."

"Please, call me Alan."

"Then it's nice to meet you, Alan." Goldfarb smiled with his perfectly white teeth.

"Come sit down." He showed them to a group of chairs and a couch. Alex wasn't surprised when he took her to a chair and sat himself directly across from her giving him a clear view of her legs. She wasn't going to disappoint him.

A man who makes pictures like the ones in the hallway would definitely want to be entertained. So, Alex adjusted her legs a few times pretending to get comfortable and let Goldfarb see what he wanted. She noticed that he was leering at her. "Well, I understand you bought a new house in Bridgehampton."

"Correct. It's a big mother of a place. I think it has over 10,000 square feet." Goldfarb again peered up Alex's skirt as he spoke.

"Sounds wonderful," Amanda commented.

"Yeah, it's great. The structure is in terrific condition, but we have to do some serious decorating. I have no furniture, so I've got to buy everything."

Alex gave him an extra special viewing opportunity and said, "That's the way we like it. Are you speaking with any other decorators?"

"No. I'm beginning the process with you. If this meeting goes well . . .," he looked at Alex hungrily, ". . . maybe we can do a deal together." Amanda observed the interplay and was a little shocked that both were so obvious about their attraction to each other. This is what she had heard about Alex Best. She was convinced that if she were not present, the two of them would already be fornicating on the couch.

They spent about 30 minutes looking at the photographs Alex brought with her, and Goldfarb was more than impressed. He liked Alex's style and liked her body even more. He appreciated Amanda's good looks as well, but Alex was marketing herself more actively and was more his type- older and sluttier.

When the business aspect of the meeting ended, Amanda asked Goldfarb about his company. Alex was surprised that Amanda dared to inquire. "So, tell us about W Pictures."

Goldfarb beamed. "To make a long story short, I'm in the soft core pornography business. We make titillating movies for adults. And yes, our movies have plots and dialogue. And no, the actors don't have actual sex. They fake it."

Alex responded, "Are the movies romantic? Do you target women as well as men?"

"Of course. We have scripts, and in them, our actors have love affairs and even get married sometimes. But, there's always an abundance of simulated sex and a fair share of grunting and screaming." Goldfarb smiled evilly.

Amanda asked, "Do you make movies in this building?"

"Sure, parts of them any way. Actually, many of the indoor scenes are filmed here. We go to exotic places such as the Caribbean for outdoor footage."

Alex queried, "Are you filming today?"

"Yes, we are. Would you like to visit a set?"

"I'm embarrassed," Amanda said shyly.

"It's no big thing. Come on, follow me."

They exited the office area of the building and entered a huge warehouse area. In it were three sets depicting a bedroom, living room and kitchen. In a far corner, a group of people was mingling about, and the lights were shining brightly.

Goldfarb led the two women to the active set. It was a bedroom scene. A younger man approached them. Goldfarb said, "Hey, big shot film director. I want to introduce you to two of the best looking women I've seen all day. Damien, meet Alex and Amanda."

"My pleasure ladies. Welcome to my set," Damien said proudly. He was particularly attracted to Amanda whose hand he shook warmly.

Goldfarb jumped in, "Damien is a new hire. He's spearheading a new movie called 'Love on a Sunny Island.' Damien, would you give Amanda a quick tour? I'd like to speak to Alex alone."

"I'd love to. Amanda, let's go over to the other side of the set."

Goldfarb said to Alex, "I received a disturbing call from Tom Gordon the other day. Frankly, he told me that you screwed him on his invoice. He claims that you overcharged him. What's that all about?"

"Alan, you're a businessman, and I'm a businesswoman. I provide quality service and demand premium prices for my work. I hate it when wealthy people have buyer's remorse especially after a job is completed, and they're satisfied with my designs."

"Alex, I'm not asking for a discount. I just don't want to get hosed. If you mess with me, you'll regret it."

"Maybe this is all a big mistake. I've got a ton of business queued up at the office. I really don't have the time or the inclination to put up with this shit. Let's forget the whole thing. I'm leaving."

"Whoa, slow down, darling. I didn't mean to insult you. I heard that your work is sensational. I want you to do my house. I'm just telling you that I don't want to get into any pissing contests down the road. You charge what you must. Just don't do anything egregious, if you know what I mean."

"Alan, you don't strike me as the kind of man who gets ripped off by anybody. And tell your buddy Tom Gordon that I will sue him for libel if I hear one more word from him."

"I'll do that. I'd like to see you alone this week to discuss the details of our relationship. Are you available?"

Alex thought the best defense is a good offense. Goldfarb couldn't resist her work or her physical attributes. The beaver shots she gave him in his office must have done the trick. "Of course. Call me with specifics."

Amanda followed Damien onto the set. They were standing in the middle of the bedroom. The sheets and blankets were all tangled up. Amanda thought that she must have just missed the real action, or was it the simulated action? Two women and one man were in bathrobes as makeup people hovered over them. There were about ten others straightening things out on the set and moving cameras and lights around.

Damien said, "The three in the robes are the principal actors. They're very popular in our business. I'm sure you haven't heard of them. The guy is I.M. Long, and the women are Natasha Sweet and Gina Sour."

Amanda responded, "Are you kidding me? Mr. Long wasn't born with that family name, was he? There must be a reason he chose 'Long.' And, the girls must be a team, sweet and sour? I guess I would have to change my name if I wanted to be in one of your movies."

Damien was snickering. "It pays to have a catchy name. And, if you ever want to try your hand at acting, give me a ring." Damien smiled broadly.

"Don't hold your breath. I think I'm going to stick with design. How old are the actors?"

"Most are in their twenties."

"They sure are a good looking crew."

"Exactly. That's why all the young guys are tuning in after 11 every night on the cable stations. They want to see naked, beautiful women. And since we don't show graphic sex, we need to employ really attractive people as a hook."

"So, there's a real science to all this."

"Yup."

"I don't know much about porn, but I hear that male performance is the key to success."

"It's not for us because you never, ever see anything but quick glimpses of male actors' private parts. And, we don't show penetration. In fact, there is no penetration permitted on our set."

"I can't believe I'm having this conversation with you," she said blushing.

"It's no big deal. We're just trying to entertain our viewers. There's nothing particularly sordid. We're depicting real relationships, but admittedly, we're trying to stimulate our audience."

"And what's the endgame?"

"To make money. A lot of money."

"How the heck did you get mixed up in this?"

"I took filmmaking courses in college and loved it."

"But why adult films?"

"I figured the odds of achieving success would be greater in this genre. Plus, I hope to make a transition to more traditional movies someday. And, one other thing, I get to meet really beautiful women."

"That's what I thought. Do you date the actresses?"

"I only started here a short time ago. But yeah, I had a couple of dates. Most of the gals are pretty nice. Many are college grads."

"Really?" Do you date normal women?"

"Normal? Sure. Maybe you and I could have dinner sometime."

"I'd like that. But, if I ever bring you home to meet my parents, you can't tell them you make dirty movies."

"Okay. If we become engaged, I'll be sure to remember that."
They laughed.

Alex and Goldfarb came strolling over. "How are you two
doing? Goldfarb asked.

"We were just discussing simulated sex," Amanda answered,
and everybody cracked up.

After more pleasantries, Goldfarb invited Alex and Amanda to
a party he was having at his new Hamptons house. He told them
it was a perfect way to celebrate, before he bought any expensive
furniture that might be destroyed if the party got out of control.
The ladies agreed to attend.

Alex had designs on Goldfarb, and Amanda was mildly interested in Damien. Before she left, Best told Goldfarb that they
might as well speak at his house, and she'd take a rain check on a
New York dinner. He concurred.

Chapter 8

That night, I decided to stay home, order some Chinese food and determine whether I had erectile disorder. I never thought I would have to pay attention to those ads for Viagra that are tele-casted during every golf tournament.

I thought about the importance of an erection in today's soci-ety. Of course, it's a prerequisite for sexual relations and child bearing. If the hydraulics don't work properly, making babies is problematic. But, the thing guys worry about most is raw sex, not sexual relations, marital bliss or any of that mushy stuff.

Getting aroused is one of the most important and fundamen-tal things in a man's life. It's his claim to fame to get hard as steel and please women. So, if anything goes awry below the belt, we go nuts, so to speak. To make matters more complicated, age has an effect on a man's performance.

The buzzer rang and I spoke with the doorman, "Yeah?"

"Your food is here, Mr. Spencer."

"Send it up." At my building all visitors had to be announced before getting on the elevator. An elevator operator accompanies deliverymen to the door. This ensures that none of the creeps who deliver food rape any female tenants.

The ability to obtain food in New York City without leaving your apartment is actually quite remarkable. Every cuisine is represented in magazine type publications that list all the restaurants that deliver food in your neighborhood. Seldom does it ever take more than an hour to arrive at your home.

The downside is the strange people who actually bring the food. I empathize with these people and usually give them over-sized gratuities. Their employers probably pay them next to nothing, which is illegal, as are most of the delivery people themselves. But honestly, the thought of one of these people handling my food makes my stomach turn.

The doorbell rang and a young Chinese man (makes sense, Chinese food, Chinese delivery man) was standing in my door-way. He was wearing a raincoat and was drenched. Through his large and water-smeared glasses, he stared at me as he handed over the ubiquitous plastic bag and waited for payment and a tip.

I took the bag, said thank you and handed him some cash. He said nothing. The tab was 50 dollars and I gave him 55 dollars. "Keep the change," I said proudly.

At last, the man spoke, "Pretty cheap missa." The elevator man was watching all this in wonderment choosing not to intervene unless it got violent.

"What's you problem?"

"Not enough tip. You cheap."

"You've got some fucking nerve. What the hell did you expect for a lousy fifty dollar Chinese dinner?"

"Not lousy food. Good food. Ten dollars better tip."

"Of course it is. But, it's twice as much as you deserve."

"You focking cheap missa."

"Get the hell out of here before I take back the five that I gave you."

"You take nottin back, missa cheap fock."

I was tempted to punch the little shit in the mouth, but he probably was a kung fu expert or a ninja. "Get lost. Sam don't let this fucker in the building ever again."

"Will do, Mr. S."

The China man stuck his head out of the elevator and said, "I wish you choke on food, cheap fock."

I slammed the door. What an ordeal for an order of General Tso's chicken and some flied lice, I mean fried rice.

The problem with America is that everyone thinks they're entitled to more money, more benefits and more time off without providing compensatory service. In fact, most service people are downright rude. People who immigrate to the United States quickly learn that the squeaky wheel gets oiled. Well, that asshole deserved five dollars, no more, no less, for this food.

I was so angry about my encounter with the deliveryman and him calling me a "cheap fock," that I decided to complain to the restaurant about their disrespectful employee.

"Order please," A young woman answered.

"I've already ordered dinner."

"It will be there soon, missa."

"My food arrived."

"What your problem, missa?"

"The deliveryman was rude."

"What rude?"

"He was obnoxious and disrespectful."

"No understand. What problem? Food okay, yes?"

"The food was fine. The delivery guy's an asshole." I decided to use some colorful words to describe the behavior of the little jerk.

"Asshole not on menu."

Exasperated, I said, "Let me speak with your boss."

"Boss no can talk. Busy in kitchen. Call later."

"Never mind." You would think that the restaurant would hire someone who could speak English to handle the call in business. I suppose they would have to pay a lot more to find someone who did.

The meal was great. Actually, I'm amazed about how many Asian restaurants there are in the City. You can spend $150 per person, before drinks, at NOBU, or you can spend 50 dollars and get your food delivered from a hole-in-the-wall joint on a nearby corner. And, they both taste delicious.

I decided to settle down and watch some porn on a cable station. For $11.95, a guy can get his rocks off without commitment, headaches, dinner or conversation. Just basic personal sex. I wondered whether W Pictures made any of these movies on the list in front of me. I thought not because these movies were explicit and the actors were having real sex. The irony is that male ejaculation is never shown on even in the most graphic movies aired on TV. I suppose it's illegal. But that was okay with me. It was the screaming and the fake orgasms that really turned me on.

I selected a film called "Beijing Princess." It was only appropriate that I watch Chinese sluts having sex after eating a delicious Chinese meal.

Well, I disrobed and made myself comfortable hoping everything would work properly. As it turns out, the movie was very hot and my body responded accordingly. I was healthy and ready to, once again, have sex with a human, preferably a female. I considered calling SS or Darla, but figured they wouldn't give a shit about my sexual rebirth.

I thought about my schedule for the next morning. I wanted to corral Rob first thing and find out whether Goldfarb was the real deal. And, I needed a date for the following evening to attend a fundraiser for the New York Designer's Foundation. I got roped into buying a table for the affair because the money collected was for a good cause- sending designers to school. Huh? What was I thinking?

Chapter 9

Jake Sardi was sitting in his rustic office at Carolina Furniture worrying about Tom Gordon. If Gordon called the pigs, it could have a domino impact on both Carolina and Best Design. He really needed to take action to prevent such a contingency. The problem was that he didn't know what kind of man Gordon was and whether he could be persuaded by angry words or the threat of physical violence.

Sardi took over Carolina ten years ago after moving from New York City, the Bronx to be exact. At the time, he was a low level punk in a large criminal family. After several bouts with the law for petty crimes such as minor extortion and assault charges, his boss felt he needed a change of venue, or he would surely end up in the federal pen.

What made Sardi so special was that he went to college, graduated and was an accountant. Understand, Sardi was well over six feet tall, a trim 215 pounds, so he was perfectly willing and capable of beating another man to death.

His crime boss in New York had made a lot of money illegally transporting guns, cigarettes and other items from the southeastern part of the country. Carolina, a small time furniture manufacturer served as an excellent front to carry untaxed and illegal merchandise to the Big Apple.

Sardi, always the entrepreneur, loyally served his New York bosses and made them a significant amount of money. He used his share of illicit gains to expand Carolina. And, about seven years ago, he met Alex Best at a trade show. He was having a drink at the hotel bar with a mutual friend. An introduction led to a very satisfying romp in the sack with Best.

Over the years, they got together to relive their first encounter and Alex always came through. Of course, business opportunities were discussed, and Alex agreed to buy more and more merchandize from Carolina for her clients. Sardi suggested a shared kickback arrangement, and they were off to the races. During the ensuing years, Sardi and Best pocketed several million dollars of overpayments from Best's wealthy clients. No one ever said a word because of the excellent service provided by Best Design, until Gordon started making a fuss.

Sardi thought a conversation with Gordon might calm him down. If not, the threat of violence would do the trick.

"Hello, Mr. Gordon's office. Can I help you?"

"It's Jake Sardi calling."

"Of course, Mr. Sardi, hold on." Two or three minutes passed and the receptionist came back on the line. "Mr. Gordon is unavailable to speak with you. Would you please give me a number where he can reach you?"

"No. Tell him he's going to be in a lot of trouble if he doesn't pick up the phone right now. It concerns our mutual friend Alexandra Best."

"I'll give him your message."

"What the hell do you want?" Gordon was agitated, perfect.

"Alex tells me you've been threatening her. That's a very bad idea, Gordon."

"You two fucked me out of six figures. Do you think I'm stupid?"

"Actually, no. But, you're so rich that we figured you wouldn't give a damn if we took a little juice from the deal. You like the merchandise, don't you?"

"Yeah, my home is beautiful. Alex did a great job. But, you two are greedy bastards."

"What do you want, Mr. Gordon? We really would be unhappy if the police became involved. In fact, it might be unhealthy for you and your family. Remember, we know where you live."

"That sounds like a threat. You don't frighten me Sardi. I just may call the authorities after I hang up."

"Well, you better prepare your wife."

"What the hell are you talking about?"

"Alex tells me that you wanted some premier service from her. You know the fucking and sucking package."

"That's bullshit. You have no proof of that."

"I'm sure your wife will understand your side of the story after we send her some pictures of you humping Alex."

Actually, what happened was that Best and Gordon decided to take pictures of each other and of themselves while they copulated. Gordon got caught up in the moment and never thought to delete them from Best's camera at the end of a very satisfying day at his new house. "Sardi, maybe you don't know whom you're dealing with. I'm a powerful man. I can destroy you, your company and Best with just a few phone calls." Gordon was really upset about being so stupid regarding the photographs.

"I can see this conversation is going nowhere. I'll send some of my associates to speak with you soon."

"You'd better not try anything. If you attempt to harm me or my family, you'll be sorry."

"Yeah sure." Sardi hung up and considered his conversation with Gordon. The man was really being shortsighted. Why didn't he just agree to forget about the overpayments? By antagonizing Sardi, he was endangering himself and his family.

Sardi made a call to a gumba from the old days, a punk in the same family that he was affiliated with. He asked if he and a buddy would do him a favor and rough Gordon up. Nothing to serious, a few punches and kicks maybe. After, he promised to send a case of Dom, the deal was set. Then, he called Alex Best.

"Ms. Best's office."

"Hi, it's Sardi. I need to speak with Alex."

"Hold on Jake."

"So, what's doing tough guy?"

"I had a conversation with Gordon. The guy's a jerk. He's not cooperating even after I threatened to hurt him and his family. Then, I said I would send those pictures you took to his wife. He damn near shit in his pants. Do you take pictures of all the men you sleep with?" He laughed.

"Look, it's a stupid thing I did. He's an okay guy. We had some fun. The camera was in my purse so we took some photos. They're very naughty, though. So what are you going to do now?"

"I'm sending a buddy and his friend to pay him a visit. They're going to slap him around."

"Oh, Jake. Is that really necessary?"

"Don't go soft on me. There's a lot at stake. Not only do I have to worry about our little scam, but I have other interests that need to be protected."

"What do you mean?"

"You don't want to know. I need those pictures Alex."

"Are you out of your mind? I'm not giving you pictures of me naked, fucking a man. Suppose they get to a newspaper or something. I would be the laughing stock of my industry."

"Okay. But, I may need them at some point." They hung up.

Best was beside herself. What the hell was Jake doing? How could he suggest she send him those pictures? She decided to put it out of her mind for the time being and see what effect Jake's buddies had on Gordon.

Chapter 10

I spent the entire morning with Rob Viand in his office discussing W Pictures. Rob indicated that W Pictures is an extremely successful company with great cash flow. A quick estimate by Rob indicated that the company, which was 100% owned by Alan Goldfarb, could be worth up to five or six hundred million dollars. Goldfarb asked Rob if he thought Pyglet could help W Pictures borrow two hundred and fifty million, which would be paid to him in the form of a dividend. Without first discussing the situation with me, Rob said the deal was feasible. I was okay with Rob's perspective and decision to move forward before obtaining my counsel. What the hell, I was busy getting my penis roughed up by my ex-wife and nearly getting beat up by Darla's Neanderthal boyfriend.

"Stoke, you have to be more focused on Pyglet. Seriously, you're the best new business guy on the planet. With the economy finally turning around, there's a ton of opportunities out there. You're only interested in your love life."

"I know. You're right. I'm not ready to retire, so I should be doing more to help everybody at the firm."

"Thanks for saying that. So, what's going on sexually? Hearing about your exploits is the most arousing thing in my life."

"Are you and Laura having issues?"

"I guess that would be an accurate assessment."

"How serious?"

"Well, we seldom have sex. And, when it does happen, she seems so tense and uninterested."

"What are you going to do? Maybe, you should get some counseling?"

"Nah. I think maybe we need a time out."

"That's really sad. I'm sorry to hear it. Do you think your marriage may be over?"

"I really think it might be. Even Laura is ready to give up."

"Have you been fooling around on the side?"

"Believe it or not, I haven't been cheating, but that's going to change real soon. In fact, I'm going out of town for a day, and perhaps I'll get lucky."

That was such an understatement. Rob is incredibly handsome, successful and charming. He could lure almost any woman into bed. And yet, his marriage was a mess. "Well, good hunting." Who am I to judge another man?

"I'm leaving right away. See you late tomorrow afternoon."

Rob left my office and I felt sad for him and Laura. Breaking up is a total bummer. And, he's such a good guy, and Laura is a doll. She's seems so depressed lately.

I had an urgent problem that I needed to deal with- no date for the charity benefit that evening. It was too late to call any of my standbys. The party was a formal affair, so it was going to be difficult to find a date who would be able to prepare herself under such time constraints.

At that moment, Laura knocked on my door and walked into my office. Rob had just departed for the airport.

"Hi Stoke. Got a minute."

"Sure. What's up?"

"Rob and I are having some problems. We're going to split. I can't waste any more of my life on him."

"What are you talking about? You two were so in love. What happened?"

"He's in love with Pyglet. He's hasn't had time for our relationship. He's also a narcissistic pig."

"That's pretty serious. Are you sure about your feelings?"

"Absolutely. I'm not angry with Rob. It's just that he needs a lot of space. And, I think he's incapable of having a long lasting relationship with one woman. He needs to play the field to feel accomplished as a man."

"I don't know what to say. What are you going to do?"

"Move on. I'm going to try to be happy again."

I felt the old feelings I had for Laura stirring inside my loins. My body was tingly and itchy as I thought about the possibilities. These were not good thoughts. The woman was vulnerable, and I certainly didn't want to get in the middle of her problems. Plus, poor judgment on my part could tear Pyglet apart.

Nevertheless, Laura looked particularly fantastic today, almost like she was moving on from her failed relationship with Rob. Maybe the impending split inspired her to dress a little more provocatively. She had on a short white skirt that was a little too short (if that's possible). And, her cotton sweater was unbuttoned a little too low (if that's possible) exposing a little too much of her ripe breasts (that's not possible). Of course, she didn't wear nylons, so I could see the contours of her beautifully tanned legs. And, her face was like an angel's. Snap out of it Stoke!

She was sitting in a chair across from me. It seems like every woman I meet with ends up in the same position, and I try to look up her dress. I couldn't tell whether she was wearing a thong. Damn it Stoke. Cool your jets. "Look, you need to think about your situation and make sure you really want to end your marriage. It's a big deal emotionally and will be very difficult with both of you in the same office."

"I know. I really don't want to do anything to upset Pyglet. I know how successful the company's been."

"I'm glad you're taking all that into consideration. I'm here for you no matter what."

Laura got up, walked over to me and kissed me lightly on the lips. Oh shit, I'm going to lose it.

"Thanks Stoke. You're a real friend."

I'm some friend. All I wanted to do was jump her right on the spot.

Liz gave me the names of the other people at my table for that evening. I didn't do anything to solicit people to sit with me, so the designer people filled my table. Among the guests were Alex Best, a top designer in the City and a trustee of the organization sponsoring the event, plus a colleague, Amanda Lane. Our other tablemates were supposed to be large donors.

Time was running short. It was five o'clock and I didn't have any brilliant ideas for a date. Then it occurred to me, what about Laura? I called Rob, who already landed. "Would you mind if I took Laura to a rubber chicken dinner tonight? I'm dateless."

"I don't give a shit. Maybe, it'll do you some good. Remember to use protection," he laughed out loud. I didn't.

"Rob, I'm not going to have sex with your wife."

"I could care less. She doesn't want me anymore."

"Thanks. Have a good trip." Boy, things were really horrible between those two. Then, I wondered whether sex was an option. Stop it Stoke. You're dreaming. I've had erotic dreams about Laura for as long as I can remember. I can't believe I didn't make love to her two years ago in my office. Liz screwed up that opportunity.

I walked over to Laura's area and told her to come into my office. I noticed that her skirt was hiked up to her upper thighs. That's the old Laura that I love so much. My God, what a fox! Her hair was long and blond and straight. I could smell her perfume. When I approached her she didn't even think to cover herself. "Be right there, Stoke."

She came in and shut the door, which was a little unusual unless she was going to tell me more about her problems with Rob. "What's going on?"

"Would you like to accompany me tonight to a fundraiser at the Plaza? I forgot to ask someone, and now it's too late. I asked Rob if it was okay with him, and he said it was fine." I decided not to tell her what he really said, about the protection and all that.

"Really, he said he had no problem with you taking me out?"

"Laura, it's not a real date. I need a woman to escort me to this stupid dinner. I spent a bundle buying a table, and it would look ridiculous if I showed up without a companion."

"I can't believe he would agree to it. If he doesn't care, it's all right with me? I'm not doing anything tonight anyway."

"It's black tie. You sure you can do it?"

"I need to leave now to get ready. But sure, I can manage it. What time? And, where should I meet you?"

"I'll pick you up at your place at seven. That'll give you more time to get ready."

"Thanks. You're so thoughtful." She left my office. I think she was dumbfounded that Rob would agree to such a crazy thing, given our history. She still wanted him to be protective of her, so allowing her go out with me was a disappointment to Laura.

I daydreamed about bringing Laura back to my place, undressing her and seeing her lying naked on my bed. She would be so tasty. Stoke, you have to stop.

Chapter 11

Alex Best and Amanda Lane were drinking coffee at about
7:30 a.m. They discussed the Goldfarb situation, and Alex told
Amanda that she wanted her to spearhead the project. Best said
she would be available for important meetings and if any problems
arose.

At first, Amanda was somewhat hesitant because she was so new
at the firm. She asked her boss if it might be too soon for her to
have so much responsibility for a job. Alex said she had total confidence in her skills. However, Alex told her that she would handle all the invoicing and payments to suppliers, something that
Amanda thought was very odd.

The subject changed to the Designer's Ball that evening. Alex
was the current Chairperson of the Designer Foundation and was
seated at a table sponsored by a man named Stoke Spencer, a big
time investment banker. The Foundation's development people
told Alex that Spencer could become an even larger benefactor,
and she should turn on the charm. Best was told privately that
Spencer was divorced. In Best's mind, when it comes to charity
causes or doing big deals nothing was out of bounds.

Best asked Lane to accompany her, as she didn't have a chance
to ask someone else to escort her. Amanda was currently unat-
tached and available so she agreed to attend. She thought it would

be fun to get dressed up and hobnob with the social elite of New York City at the Plaza Hotel.

Amanda asked Alex, "So, what are you wearing tonight?"

"Well, I have to be decked out because I'm hosting the affair and giving a speech to the attendees. So, I bought a Valentino a few weeks ago. I'm going to be showing a lot of skin for this cause. The Foundation head told me that I was supposed to do whatever I could to get the people sitting at our table to give more money. The dress should be perfect for the seduction." Both women cracked up.

"Tell me more. How long is it? What color? Is it strapless?"

"It's a floor length, blood red gown. No straps. Straps would make it too easy for me to keep my boobs from jumping out of the dress. That's no fun. Anyway, if the attendees had a chance to see my tits, it would be a gigantic boon for the Foundation." The woman laughed again.

Amanda looked at Best's breasts and admired them. For sure, she paid enough money to a plastic surgeon so that their public display wouldn't disappoint any of the men, or the women for that matter. "You have a great figure. All the men, I'm sure, would love to see those beauties."

"Why thank you. Would you like to see them? My surgeon actually took pictures of my boobs to show prospective patients."

"I don't know what to say. Sure, I'd love to see them, I guess."

Best pulled off her sweater and unclasped her bra, exposing her prides and joy. "Aren't they gorgeous?"

"They are perfect. I envy you. I'm too small for my body size."

Best ignored her comment and said, "Would you like to feel them?"

"I don't think so."

"Come on. Touch them. They're just firm enough. Go ahead."

"I'd feel strange doing that."

"This isn't a sexual encounter. I'm just showing you my tits. Touch them."

"Okay." Amanda touched one of the breasts for a nanosecond and tried to back off.

Best grabbed her hand and forced her to have a real feel. "Touch me like a man would. That's the whole purpose of having your chest redone. They are supposed to felt by others." Amanda followed Best's orders, and they were amazing, firm and yet supple at the same time.

"Wow. I don't know what to say." Best got dressed.

"So what are you wearing tonight?"

"I have a boring little short, black sequined dress that I bought at Bergdorf, no designer stuff for me. It's very cute but not anything as glamorous as what you're wearing."

"I'm sure you will look beautiful. It's my turn to feel your tits." Amanda didn't know what to say. "Only kidding. Please Amanda, relax."

"For a moment, I thought you were serious," Amanda giggled nervously.

"Is the dress sexy?"

"It's about knee length, but low cut. However, I don't have any breast risk. It's revealing enough for me."

Best responded, "Sounds great." She really didn't give a shit about Amanda's dress. However, she would like to see Amanda naked.

"Do you have some great jewelry to wear with your gown?"

"As a matter of fact, I borrowed a diamond necklace from my jeweler. It's absolutely amazing. I'll have to work until I'm 100, if I lose it."

The coffee klatch ended and both women went to work.

. . .

In the meantime, two of Jack Sardi's pals were planning to have a chat with Tom Gordon. Gordon commuted in from Greenwich, Connecticut to New York City every morning on the same train. He was a senior executive at a large leveraged buyout firm located in Midtown. The two men ascertained that Gordon's train was arriving in Grand Central Station just before nine on track number 21. They were waiting at the top of the stairs that overlooked the track. Both had memorized a photograph of their target. The assignment was to scare the crap out of Gordon. They were told that Jake's beef with the man had something to do with a furniture deal, not that it mattered.

The two thugs were soldiers in a Mafia family that controlled a wide range of illegal activities in Manhattan and Brooklyn. These men often conducted this type of operation as part of a large extortion business. Nobody is supposed to get hurt seriously during his or her first encounter with an enforcer.

Gordon was one of the first passengers up the stairs. The senior wise guy figured that Gordon was a type A kind of guy, always rushing all over the place.

As he passed by, the senior man said, "Are you Tom Gordon?"

Gordon was surprised to hear his name, especially from such a large scary looking man. "Yes. Who are you?"

"Jake Sardi is a good buddy of ours. He said you were fucking with him."

"You better not start any trouble. There are a lot of cops in the terminal."

"We don't want any trouble. We just wanted to talk to you." The second man blocked Gordon as he tried to slip away and herded him against the wall on the main concourse.

"Don't hurt me. I warn you."

"Shut the fuck up, you pussy."

"What do you want from me?"

"Jake told us you were going to make trouble for him, that you were going to talk to the cops. That wouldn't be a good idea. You better just pay your debt to Jake or we just might come back and really fuck you up."

"I'm going to the police if you lay a hand on me."

"Do you really think you can frighten us with the police? I don't think so. And, if you yak to the cops, we might come up to Connecticut to visit your wife and kids."

"You're just two punks. I'm not going to take any more of this shit. Get out of my way."

The senior man looked at the junior man and nodded. Like a bolt of lightening, junior punched Gordon in the solar plexus. The blow took his breath away, and he doubled over in pain. Senior stood in the way so no one could see what was happening. Gordon started to cough up his coffee and bagel. "Do you understand that we mean business Mr. Gordon?" He shook his head, and the men walked away.

Gordon staggered to his office. He considered what had just taken place. It appears that Jake Sardi and Alex Best weren't going to back off and wanted their money. He decided to give Alex a call.

"Ms. Best's office. Can I help you?"

"I'd like to speak with her please. It's Tom Gordon."

"Hello Tom. How are you?" It was Alex.

"Not so great. I just got beaten up by some of Jake Sardi's pals. Do you know anything about this?"

"That's horrible." Best giggled silently. Apparently, Jake was taking the low road. This really didn't' surprise Best. "I guess he's upset you refused to pay your bill and threatened to go to the police."

"I still may do that even though those thugs said they would harm my family."

"I don't know anything about that. Why don't you just send me a check, and we can drop this whole thing. And besides, I shook your world, didn't I?"

"Alex you're a beautiful woman and a great piece of ass, but money is money. And those fuckers beat me up."

"Think about it, Tom. If you pay up, maybe we can get together again for a night on the town."

"I'll get back to you."

Alex cracked up. What a dope. He's filthy rich and still insists on endangering his family for a lousy two hundred grand or so. Oh well, some guys will never learn.

Chapter 12

As I got dressed for the evening's affair, I considered the implications of taking Laura to the Designer's Ball. It was a very dangerous move even though Rob knew about the plan and signed off on it. If I acted irresponsibly, I might seriously damage my relationship with him.

Ever notice how guys react after they split with wives and girlfriends? When their exes go on dates or begin a new relationship, their former partners are very jealous even if they hate their exes. The thought of another person sleeping with a former lover is too much to bear.

I was different, however. I'd be ecstatic if SS hooked up with a rich stud so I could stop paying alimony. I wouldn't hold it against her if she fell madly in love with another man. I should consider offering a bounty to any man who takes SS off my hands.

My date with Laura, as innocent as it seems, could be the final straw that brings down Rob and Laura's marriage. Do I really want to have that hanging over me?

Then, I thought, what the hell's the big deal? I'll pick up Laura, we'll eat our rubber chicken, I'll bring her home and we'll make love the entire night. Oops, I didn't mean that. I'll just bring her home, kiss her on the cheek and go home and masturbate. That's a more likely scenario.

And besides, Laura is going to have something to say about all this. Even if I want to sleep with her, it doesn't mean she's going to jump into my bed. It takes two to tango. Otherwise, it's rape. But, suppose she wants some affection. Will I be able to resist her? Probably not, I speculated.

I guarantee that Laura is going to look fabulous tonight, and I will have to do everything in my power not to have unclean thoughts. And, what if she comes on to me? Suppose she grabs my balls on the way to the ball? I'll bet that would really ball me up.

Liz hired a limousine to take us to the event. She figured out that I was taking Laura out and had serious misgivings. I assured her that I wasn't going to relive the last encounter, in which Laura wanted to have sex, I agreed, Liz broke it up and I got sued for sexual harassment. No way was I going down that path again.

Was I trying to impress Laura with the limo? Yes, of course. Would the spacious limo enable me to hump Laura if I had the opportunity? Yes. Stop it Stoke. You're going to do the wrong thing tonight unless you clear your mind about this woman. She's a friend, that's all.

When Liz walked in on Laura and me just as I was about to hit pay dirt, everything went sour. Liz called me every name in the book and Laura hired a lawyer. I must learn from these experiences. I must protect myself.

But, to finally connect with Laura and wallow in her beauty has always been my dream. She would be my ultimate conquest. All I need to do is get over the fact that I would be hitting on my best friend's wife.

And, one more thing, is Laura even remotely interested in me? She's married to a wealthy man, who I made rich, by the way. Her husband is one of the most macho and best-looking guys in New York City. Does she want to sleep with a fifty-something year old has-been?

. . .

At the same time, Alex Best was getting ready at her place. She couldn't get her mind off Amanda. What a counter point she was. Tall, willowy, young and innocent, perhaps, perhaps not. Usually, Best didn't get all worked up about other women because she was mostly heterosexual. But, the opportunity to kiss every inch of Amanda's smooth white skin, and have her return the favor, was making her wild with anticipation.

They'd only been working together for a few days, and Amanda had shown not one scintilla of interest in Best from a physical point of view. But, maybe she's shy, maybe she's a raging heterosexual, maybe she's scared to death of her new boss. Unless Amanda had previous experiences with women, she will be difficult to conquer.

Best knew she had an ace in the hole; she was Amanda's boss. Sexual domination when you are in charge financially was a great advantage, even if it was technically illegal. What the hell could Amanda do if Best came on to her, and she wasn't interested? Nothing, unless Best got too aggressive and domineering. Sometimes determination gets you where you want to be in a sexual situation.

She thought, we'll see what happens. Maybe, Amanda will have a few glasses of wine and loosen her up. And, anything might be possible in the confines of a stretch limousine.

. . .

Laura went home early to get ready for her date with Stoke. No, she thought, that's not the right way to describe the evening. She was only doing an old friend a favor. He needed someone to take to a charity dinner. That's all.

But, what if the evening evolves into another opportunity for them to be physical. For years, Stoke had drooled over her. Long before she married Rob, Stoke would seek opportunities to peak at her legs if she wore a short skirt, or look down her blouse if it was loose fitting. At the time, Laura was flattered that powerful men were so interested in her. Even when they called her "the thong" behind her back, it didn't really bother her.

Over the years, the fraternity-like behavior got on her nerves, but she never really took it personally. She was beautiful and dressed provocatively most of the time, so it was no big deal. When she started dating Rob secretly, everything changed.

Their affair was steamy, exciting and everything she dreamed about how it would be to fall in love. The only problem was that Rob was a confirmed bachelor, and there was no way he could bring home a blonde to his very Greek family. As their relationship intensified, Laura became more and more frustrated, and she began to place increasing pressure on Rob to take the next step. It came to a climax one fateful late night at Pyglet.

Laura approached Stoke in his office after every other employee had gone home. She confided in Stoke about her relationship with Rob, which was not progressing as she had hoped. One thing led to the next, and soon both undressed. Right before the moment, Liz came in after a long night on the town and broke up the liaison. Afterwards, Laura accused Stoke of sexual harassment.

Was Laura prepared to take the next step in dismantling her marriage? Was Stoke the right person to get involved with romantically? She needed to think about these and other issues as the night progressed. She found it difficult to believe that Stoke wouldn't make a play for her affection.

. . .

Amanda Lane wasn't inexperienced sexually. In college, she dated several men and slept with a few of them. She never felt like she was really in love with any man in her life. But, in most cases, her experiences were pleasurable and often times erotic and exciting. After graduation, Lane dated, but after five years, she didn't have a steady boyfriend. She immersed herself in her work.

Tonight, Lane was Alex Best's date. That didn't necessarily mean it would be a sexual adventure, but she felt just a bit strange.

Given what happened earlier in the day with Best's breasts, and the way she ogled her from time to time, Lane knew something could happen. And, she needed to be prepared because it could impact her career.

To her knowledge, Best wasn't gay. In fact, she dated many famous unmarried and married men if one believed the gossip columns. But, powerful women like Best were unpredictable, and their appetites could change on a dime. She wouldn't be surprised if Best came on to her at some point. In the business of design, gay relationships and bi-sexual relationships were commonplace and aren't considered to be in bad taste.

Lane had dabbled with a couple of women over the years, primarily in college. At the time, too much alcohol and revelry could result in a shared bed with a friend, a female friend. And, in the moment, some heavy petting might take place. Only once did such an episode really get interesting. Admittedly, it was very stimulating and resulted in unexpected and explosive orgasms for her and her partner. Afterwards, nothing was ever said, and the girls went back to their boyfriends du jour. Ironically, Amanda was maid of honor in her lover's wedding to a man a few years later.

So, if Best made a move, she needed to have a plan. At this early stage of her business relationship with Best, Amanda thought she should respectfully say thanks, but no thanks.

Chapter 13

The crew for Goldfarb's latest flick assembled at the studio at noon. Two female actors and one male actor would be filmed today. Catering was serving food to everyone as they awaited Goldfarb's arrival.

In his office, Goldfarb was lecturing Damien about the ins and outs of the business. "You must remember that most of the actors are morons aspiring to be in legitimate cinema. They do everything possible to get their faces on camera hoping to be discovered."

"What do you mean," Damien inquired.

"The females, in particular, will always try to have the cameras focus on their faces not their tits and asses. They think they're going to be discovered by a producer who's watching one of our movies late at night. These people are diluted and don't understand that making a transition from our genre to 'Gone with the Wind' is virtually impossible."

"Oh heck. I understand their motivations. All the pretty girls want to act in a great movie, attend the Oscars and be interviewed by *People Magazine*."

"What I'm trying to tell you is that you have to be tough with these people. Don't let them jerk you around. You're the boss."

"I understand." Damien was a little disappointed that Gold-farb was so negative about the staff. After all, they were making him a lot of money.

"Your job is to tease and excite the viewers. You'll have a lot to work with. I'm sure you've noticed that most of the actors are very attractive. You must take advantage of their looks and make the films really sexy without filming actual sex. It's not that easy to do. Do you understand?"

"Yes boss." Damien thought, what was the sense in expressing any opinions? Goldfarb was set in his ways and method of doing business. And, based upon his net worth, who could argue with the man?

"I want you to have a really good time. After filming, you might want to have a private meeting with one of the actresses who will be more that happy to shake your world for another opportunity."

"I can't wait for that." They both laughed.

"Let's get going. Everyone's waiting for us."

The pair made the long walk to the bedroom studio. When they arrived, Goldfarb hollered, "Okay people, let's do something really erotic." The crew responded enthusiastically. Morale was high on the set.

Goldfarb was going to direct this scene personally. "Diane, I want you to enter the room and approach Sam. You're going to start bitching about Sam constantly ogling Jenna, per the script. Ready? Action."

Diane strode in wearing a bikini and a see through cover over her bottom. It was floral. She was really putting on a show and smiling way too much for a woman who was supposed to be pissed off.

"Cut. No Diane. You're supposed to be scowling. You're angry about Sam wanting to fuck your best friend."

"Sorry Alan."

"Do it right. Action."

Once again, Alan wasn't happy with Diane's portrayal of a woman scorned. "What the fuck is wrong with you? This is a simple scene. Be angry, please."

Diane finally got it right on the third try.

Damien was watching carefully and was really attracted to Diane, a petite little blonde with surgically created breasts that were oversized and stuck straight out.

After a few minutes of arguing, Diane and Sam started to make out and feel each other up. The dialogue ended, and it was all grope and grunt from that point on. Soon Sam undid Diane's bra and two of the most beautiful boobs were exposed. Damien felt a surge of testosterone. He was embarrassed that he was aroused by what was taking place.

Sam was kissing Diane's breasts enthusiastically. From the bulge in his bathing suit, he was also getting off on Diane's hot little body.

The sex scene progressed as it usually does. Diane kissed Sam all over, Sam kissed Diane all over and now they were simulating intercourse. All this time, the cameras were carefully avoiding Sam's genitalia. However, the censors would allow quick glimpses of Diane's pubic area.

Suddenly, there was a knock at the door, and Jenna walked in, also clad in a bikini. What else? By this time, Diane and Sam had changed sexual positions several times. Damien was getting more turned on and asked himself how simulated sex could possibly move him. Then, he remembered what Goldfarb had said earlier about the women being so attractive. Somehow, the action was a turn on even though it was make believe. Viewers wouldn't be able to tell whether the sex was real either, but hopefully, they would get excited.

Back to the film, Diane was furious that Jenna barged in, but continued getting it on with Sam, who was now very aroused, something that would not be seen on film. Jenna asked if she could join them in bed. Sam enthusiastically supported that suggestion. Jenna stripped and was a perfect counterpoint to Diane. Her hair was brunette and in a ponytail; she was almost six feet tall in heels; and her ass was almost twice as large as Diane's. But, she was gorgeous and perfectly proportioned.

The filming only lasted a few more moments because of the difficult camera angles. How you can film two women and a man rolling around together, pretending to have sex, and not show any penis is no small feat.

"Cut and print it." Alan was pleased with what he saw, especially after having to scold Diane so many times. "Everybody, take 30 minutes. Diane, I want to see you privately." She donned a bathrobe and followed Goldfarb.

Damien approached Jenna, who was still completely naked. She was almost as tall as he with her three-inch heels. "Nice job, Jenna. You looked really beautiful in the scene," he said as he looked at her bare breasts. They were huge, yet magnificent. He couldn't believe he was chatting with a nude woman while so many other people were hanging around.

"Thanks Damien. How are you enjoying your new job at the company?"

"How could it be better? I get to meet beautiful women like you every day."

"You're sweet. We should have a drink together sometime."

"You date people you work with?"

"Why not? You're a handsome guy. We could have some fun."

"I'd like that. You sure are beautiful."

"I gotta get dressed. I'll see you around."

"Bye." Damien had a smile on his face as he headed back to his office. In route, he passed by the darkened living room set and saw Goldfarb and Diane rolling around together. He was ravaging the woman, but she didn't seem to be a willing participant. Damien hid behind a curtain and watched lustfully, even though he felt guilty doing so.

"Stop Alan. You're being too rough. Somebody might see us."

"Shut up and do what I tell you." He tried to force Diane to touch his private parts, but she resisted, so he began to strong-arm her. Diane began to choke and cry. "Just do it."

"Please Alan, I don't want to do this." He then threw her down on the couch and tried to mount her.

She screamed out, "Stop, you're hurting me."

Alan continued to thrust into her, and soon it became too violent for Damien to just stand by. "Alan, what the hell are you doing?"

"Get out of here Damien. I'm busy."

"Diane said she wants you to stop. You better end this before it goes too far."

"If you don't mind your own business, you'll be in trouble." Suddenly, Diane escaped Goldfarb's grip and ran off.

"Take it easy boss. You were getting out of control."

"When I'm busy in the future, you'd best stay away. If you ever interrupt me again, your career will be over." Goldfarb pulled up his pants and stormed off to his office.

Damien caught up with Diane. "Are you okay?"

"Yeah, I'm all right. Alan just got a little carried away. He does that sometimes."

Jenna approached. "That's right, Alan gets a little crazy sometimes after he directs a sex scene. He thinks he can fuck us whenever he wants."

"You don't have a problem with that?"

Jenna responded, "How can we? First of all, we fuck in films, sort of. Second, he'll throw us off the set if we don't do what he wants."

Damien walked away wondering what kind of monster he was working for.

Chapter 14

I was on my way to pick up Laura in a stretch limousine. What the hell, I wasn't going to spare any expense tonight. The vehicle was equipped with a bar, television and privacy shield that could isolate us from the driver. I received a full briefing from the pilot of the limo before taking off. He seemed like a nice guy, who understood my intentions, even if I didn't.

The car pulled up to Laura's building on Central Park West, an old and prestigious edifice. I paid Rob a ton of money enabling him to afford such expensive real estate. I thought it would be too presumptuous to go up to Laura's place, so I told the doorman to ring her apartment and tell her I was waiting.

As I sat there, I, once again, contemplated what could happen this evening. From my perspective, an opportunity to feast on Laura was something I was going to have a difficult time resisting. But what about the morality of it all?

If Rob and Laura's marriage was over, I should be able to make a play for this gorgeous woman. Right? But, I couldn't justify becoming part of their problems. I needed to wait until it played out before attempting anything. Even then, dating Laura would have repercussions in the office. For one thing, I'd have to tell Liz, who might beat the crap out of me.

So, I had a plan. Be cool and make no aggressive moves. If Laura made an advance . . . oh hell, I don't know what I'd do. Then again, she probably wouldn't succumb to me on our first "date".

All of a sudden she appeared. Unbelievable. The woman of my dreams was before me. She had on a blue dress to mid calf. It was that airy type material, so the breeze outside blew the dress in different directions as she approached the car. She looked like a ballerina. Around her neck, she had a string of pearls, a large string that circumnavigated her neck twice, and yet, it fell below her partially exposed breasts. Her blond hair was up, not in a tight formal way. It was done more casually. Honest, the woman looked like a runway model.

The driver scrambled around the car and opened the door for my date. I slid over and watched her get in focusing on her increasingly exposed legs. She was so graceful. "You look ravishing."

"Thanks Stoke. You look very distinguished in your tuxedo."

I guess that was a compliment. "I hope it wasn't too much of an inconvenience for you to come tonight. I asked you so late in the day. But, you really did rally. Oh my God, I must be with a movie star?"

"It was no big deal. I bought a few nice dresses anticipating that Rob and I would attend some formal affairs. We haven't, so the dresses have been collecting dust in my closet. I'm so glad to go out with you. It should be fun."

Hint, hint. Big trouble with Rob. He doesn't ever take her out. He's either too busy at work, or he really doesn't want to be with Laura. If I were married to this woman, I probably wouldn't have the energy to go out. I'd be in bed with her every chance and be too sore to walk. "Yes, we're going to have a lot of fun tonight. I don't congregate with these artistic types very often, so it should be interesting to say the least. Alexandra Best will be seated with us. She's a famous home designer and the host for the evening. Have you ever heard of her?"

"I think I have. She's in the gossip columns quite often as I recall. She's frequently seen with famous and very handsome men."

"You look lovely tonight."

"Stop it Stoke. You're making me blush."

We drove south on Central Park West, veered around Columbus Circle and headed east on 59th Street towards the Plaza. It was a short drive, and we arrived early. I don't like spending too much time at cocktail receptions because I drink too much. And, when I have too much wine, I get tipsy and a little frisky. "Laura, we're too early. Would you like to take a quick walk in the Park?"

"I'm wearing high heels, so not too long of a walk, okay?"

"Sure. We crossed at the corner of 59th and Fifth and settled down on an empty bench. "This okay?"

"Perfect. Thanks for not hiking too far. Women's designer shoes are not made for trekking. That's for sure. They make them so pointy that our toes get squished in the front of the shoes. Our feet get real sore, real fast."

"I never understood why women buy uncomfortable high heels. I suppose they make their legs seem longer, but I really could care less."

"Most women dressed to be admired by other women. Although, we know that men want us to look sexy. Some of my female friends believe it's better to look good than feel good."

"That's very funny. And, by the way, you're absolutely correct. Men like hot clothes. Personally, I like no clothes."

"Ha, ha, ha. Very funny."

"So what's really going on between you and Rob?"

"You always seem to be in the middle of my private affairs. I can still vividly remember the last time I confided in you."

"Yeah, me too. That was a disaster. You really were pissed at me."

"At you and Rob, actually."

"You wanted to get married. You were in love. Sometimes people do crazy things when their love lives are in turmoil."

"Well, I did come on to you. Sorry about that."

"I wasn't unhappy that you did. I was disappointed that you sued me afterwards even though nothing transpired."

Her face lit up and she began to laugh. "Can you believe it, I sued you, and we didn't even have sex? That was unfair. I admit it."

"You're damn right it was." I laughed with her. "But, what about now?"

"My marriage is going downhill. I love Rob, but it's impossible for him to be in love with one woman. Frankly, he loves Pyglet too much, and he's currently unhappy being with me."

"Is he cheating on you?" Deep down, I hoped Rob was cheating, so that it wouldn't be so terrible if Laura and I hooked up tonight. I felt guilty that this crossed my mind yet another time.

"You keep him so busy that he doesn't have the time for an affair unless he's seeing other women at lunch."

"I hadn't thought about that. Do you think he wants to see other women?"

"Yes. But, I think he's been loyal to me up to now."

"Wow. So what are you going to do? Are you planning to see a marriage counselor?

"No, Rob would never do that. He's too cool and macho for that."

"So, is it over?"

"Yes, I believe it is."

"How do you feel about me?"

"Honestly, you're like a big brother."

Shit, I hate that. I don't want to be her big brother. I want to be her sugar daddy.

"I don't know if we can ever have a romantic relationship."

Shit, shit, shit.

I had no choice but to play it straight, and so I said, "I want to be there for you." When you need sex, I want to provide it, I thought to myself. "It's going to be difficult at Pyglet, but we must separate business from personal issues."

"Yes. That's right. However, I will quit if you want me to."

"That won't be necessary." I lied because the thought of not seeing Laura every day was too much for me to bear. I admitted to myself that it probably would be the right thing for Pyglet.

Laura leaned over to me and kissed me hard on the lips. She opened her mouth and invited me in. My head was spinning. I was blown away by her soft skin and intoxicating perfume.

I said, "What was that all about?"

"I'm not sure what to do, so I want to keep all my options open."

"Laura, Rob is my friend and partner."

"I know. This all needs to be handled with great sensitivity no matter who ends up with who."

"I hate love triangles."

"Oh please, Stoke. Don't be so melodramatic. If we ever do make love, you'll probably be disappointed after so many years of anticipation and fantasizing about me."

"You are so wrong. You see this pinky. I would cut it off to see you walk around in a thong."

Laura went hysterical. "'The thong.' By the way, I'm wearing a tiny black thong tonight. Maybe you'll get lucky and see it later in the evening."

"Let's get out of here before I have an accident in my pants." Laura laughed again. But, I wasn't kidding.

• • •

Best also hired a stretch limousine and sent it to pick up Amanda. On the way to her boss's building, Amanda considered her current situation. She was 26 years old, a graduate of Yale, had five years experience in the design business and no serious boyfriends for quite some time.

She thought, what the hell is wrong with me? I'm great looking, articulate and can party with the best of them. Unfortunately, her business ambition and success to date made it difficult for her to meet men, straight men anyway. And, she wasn't one to go to bars to find love.

There was one man about a year ago who Amanda believed could be an excellent prospect. After dating and sleeping together, Amanda concluded that he really wasn't her equal intellectually. Moreover, he had a bit of a mean streak. In fact, after a night of arguing about the direction of their relationship, he pushed her around some. That's an automatic death sentence in Amanda's mind, and so the relationship ended immediately.

The car approached Alex's place, and Amanda decided to have fun tonight and maybe drink several glasses of wine. Some available, attractive and wealthy men might be at the gala. What the hell, she might as well go for a triple play.

The doorman asked whom the limo was to pick up, and after being informed it was Best, he called her apartment. In about fifteen minutes, Best made her way out of the building. Amanda was a little annoyed that Best made her wait so long. She was such a self-centered person.

Best's outfit stunned Amanda. She looked absolutely amazing. Her long gown was beautiful. And, adorned with a million dollars worth of "borrowed" necklaces and earrings, the woman was a knockout.

"Oh my God, you look fantastic."

"Why thank you Amanda. It must be the jewels."

"No ma'am. It's your dress, your figure and your face. Well-done boss. You will turn some heads tonight."

"Love your get up as well. I bet the men will be ogling you as well."

"I'm not in your league."

"Now, all I have to do is make sure my body parts stay in the dress. I don't need a Janet Jackson malfunction. If I have too much to drink, keep me off the dance floor because I may expose myself if I get too into the music." They both laughed.

The ride to the Plaza lasted only a few minutes, so the conversation was not extended. Amanda wondered whether Best would make a play for a man tonight. She certainly had that reputation.

Chapter 15

Laura and I entered the grand ballroom and were escorted to the dance floor. Several people from the Designer Foundation approached me and thanked me for my generous contribution.

The place was decorated exquisitely. Ten people were assigned to each table. Magnificent dinnerware and a unique centerpiece adorned each position. Flowers on vines were draped across the room 30 feet above giving the ballroom a grotto-like feeling.

Laura said to me, "You must have given the organization a large gift. They're treating you like royalty."

"Maybe I gave too much. It's amazing how you can acquire the admiration of others by writing large checks. Hell, I never even heard of this organization until a few weeks ago. I don't know what hell came over me, but I just decided to be generous."

"Well, I think it was very nice of you."

"Thanks."

Laura had her arm through mine as we searched for our seats. Each table had cards indicating where everybody should sit. Otherwise, a gigantic musical chairs scene would result as the guests tried to organize the seating themselves.

I looked at the seating assignments at our table and saw that Alexandra Best, the Chairwoman of the Designer Foundation, was next to me. Best had not yet arrived. I expected a frumpy middle aged, rich bitch to appear. Boy, was I surprised to see her for the first time.

Suddenly, at the entrance to the ballroom, flashbulbs were popping as a large gaggle of people huddled around someone. A major celebrity must have arrived, I thought. Through the crowd, a gorgeous woman in red came into view. She was smiling for the crowd and accepting the accolades of the attendees. Soon, she was standing beside me. I was flabbergasted.

"Hello, I'm Alexandra Best. Call me Alex. You must be the wonderful, generous and wealthy Stoke Spencer.

I like that, the wonderful, generous and wealthy Stoke Spencer. "I'm honored to be here."

"You gave enough money. You earned your invitation." We smiled at each other.

I thought to myself, what would this woman be like in bed? I bet she was a total vixen, only interested in her own gratification. So what's wrong with that? "You look amazing Alex. This is my good friend Laura Palmer."

"Nice to meet you Ms. Best."

"Please, it's Alex."

"Okay Alex."

Best quickly turned away from Laura. She must have considered her to be competition. I love when women fight for the right to mate with me.

Best said, "Shall we be seated" to everyone at the table.

I thought it was rude that Best didn't introduce me to her companion, a woman. I immediately wondered whether Best was gay. So, I introduced myself to the lady. "Hi, I'm Stoke Spencer."

"Nice to meet you, I'm Amanda Lane."

What a fox, I thought. The woman was beautiful and graceful. I wondered whether Alex would be getting it on with her after the party. I'd love to witness that event. Sitting next to three fabulously great looking women was overwhelming.

"Do you work with Alex?" Or are you her sex toy?

"Yes I do. We are home designers."

"Oh, I know that."

Best interrupted us after she finished acknowledging yet another admirer. "And what is your relationship with Laura?"

Well, I hope to engage in wild passionate sex with her after we leave this rubber chicken dinner waste of time. I would be happy to sleep with either you or Amanda as well. "Laura and I are colleagues." The jousting was underway as we sized each other up.

"Colleagues where?

"An investment bank."

"What's the company's name?"

"Pyglet."

"How interesting. What's the derivation of the name?

"It's a long story."

"Maybe you can tell me about it sometime. How long have you worked there, Stoke?"

"Since I founded it a few years ago."

"Oh, sorry." She wasn't really.

"What's the name of your company? I'm not up to speed on designer firms." I asked.

"Best Design, of course."

"Of course it is."

The woman was good looking, but she was an obnoxious bitch. I hated her after being in her company for just a few moments. Nevertheless, she reeked of raw, uninhibited and selfish sex.

I turned away and started chatting with Laura and the couple next to her. They weren't married either. Both were on the board of the Designer Foundation. We spoke about the mission of the organization, in which I could have cared less. This was the problem with events such as these. You spend a fortune, become totally bored with inane conversation and then eat a lousy meal. I should've bagged the dinner and taken Laura to the Four Seasons. After putting up with all this nonsense and social sparring, I should at least get laid tonight. Calm down, Stoke!

The evening proceeded, and every ten seconds somebody stopped by to speak with Best, and frankly, to kiss her ass. It was so annoying. I couldn't eat my disgusting meal in peace. So much for sitting at the table of honor.

About an hour into the affair and just after the cold filet mignon (it was supposed to be hot), Best got up without excusing herself and walked to the stage. Oh great, a bitch speech.

After she left, I leaned over to Amanda and said, "Is she always so full of herself?"

Amanda started to giggle, much to my surprise. "What a question? Should I tell Alex what you said?" She was smiling beautifully.

"You can tell Alex anything you want. But, I was only kidding. I suppose she's a little wound up tonight because she has to make a speech."

"Nice try, Stoke. Don't worry. I won't say anything. She's is acting like she has a stick up her ass."

Now, I started to laugh. "I like you Miss Lane. Can I ask you a personal question?"

"We aren't a couple, and we aren't lovers."

"I wasn't going to ask that."

"Maybe you weren't, but that's what you were thinking."

"Okay, you got me. I'm so happy you aren't gay."

"I didn't say I wasn't gay. What's wrong with being gay?"

"Nothing. There are usually scads of gay people at these events."

She smiled, ending the uneasy give and take.

Laura said to me quietly, "Stoke, please, be more discreet when saying things that might offend others."

"Sorry."

"Can I have your attention?" It was Best about to deliver her pitch.

"Good evening, I'm Alexandra Best, the Chairperson of the Designer Foundation." Many people started clapping and whistling. "It's my honor tonight to serve as the host for this grand affair at the beautiful and newly redesigned Plaza Hotel for which I was not hired." Everyone laughed.

"I'm delighted to tell you that your generosity tonight will increase the coffers of the Design Foundation by over $2.5 million. And, the night's still young. Maybe I can convince a few of you big spenders to increase your pledges. The economy is starting to turn around, right?"

Somebody yelled out, "It's still not good, Alex."

"Oh come on. This is charity. Don't be a bunch of cheap-skates. In fact, I will have dinner with any one of you who increases your pledge by $100,000."

I thought, who does this woman think she is, Gwyneth Paltrow? Who the hell wants to eat with her? If she offered to have sex with me in a hotel room and not say one word the entire time, I might consider increasing my donation. Screaming in ecstasy would be permissible and desireable, however.

"This is your chance to help up and coming designers obtain training so one day they will be able to rip you off as they redecorate your homes." I heard a few snickers. The woman was bombing.

"Now I'd like to thank a few people for putting together this wonderful party . . ."

Thank goodness the speech finally ended. I was really embarrassed for Best. I decided to take a walk to the men's room just as the band started to play some old fart music.

As I searched for the toilets, I saw a few people I knew and shook their hands. Finally, relief.

As is commonplace, an attendant was present to insure that nobody used too many paper towels. You're pressured into paying these guys for turning on the water. They usually make a comment about sports or how sharp you look to encourage your generosity. I didn't have any problems with the custom and usually put five dollars in the tip jar.

The man at the adjacent urinal and I finished at the same moment. I walked to the sink, and he walked out the door. I finished quickly and ran after the slob.

"Hey pal. You forgot to wash your hands. Didn't your mama tell you to clean yourself after you touch your dick?"

"Excuse me."

"You didn't wash after you pissed."

"What's your problem?" He was a small man in his mid fifties. I didn't feel threatened physically.

"You're a pig. That's my problem. If you were at my table, I'd tell everyone not to make contact with you."

The guy started to shake his head and walked away. If there's anything that makes me crazy, it's people who use the toilet and don't rinse off.

I started back and literally bumped into Alex Best. "Sorry."

She said, "You should watch where you're going."

"I said I was sorry. You want me to get down on my knees and beg for forgiveness?" I didn't know whether she was kidding or not.

"So how did you like my speech?"

"Actually, I think you need a new writer."

"You didn't approve of something I said?"

"Well, you were a little pushy about giving more money."

"That's how you raise money in this town."

"I don't think it's appropriate. It's a good thing you already have my check."

"Wow. That's pretty harsh."

The woman was fighting back, but she really didn't care what I had to say. Sometimes, I'm a little too blunt.

"Well, why don't you call me? I'd like you to tell me how you would've addressed the group. And, maybe I can get you to give more money to the Foundation." She winked at me.

Now we were getting someplace. I don't want to be friends with Alex, but I'd love to see her naked. "I just might give you a ring. Maybe we can teach each other a few things."

"I'm sure I will have you screaming for more."

Great, a new opportunity. You're probably thinking to yourself, he just said he hated this woman. Why is he encouraging another encounter? I believe all sexual opportunities should be pursued especially when the target is a woman who looks like Alex Best.

Laura and I danced a few times and chatted while we held each other. She was lovely, soft and smelled wonderful. I hope she didn't notice that I was slightly aroused when we were close to each other. I think maybe she did because she pushed her hips into me.

Thankfully, the event came to a close. I said goodbye to Amanda who basically sat in her seat the entire night while Best skulked around the room propositioning men for more donations. "Good night Amanda. Looks like this was a pretty lousy evening for you."

"Part of the job."

"Well, you're a very nice person. You should find yourself a big stud, get married and have children."

"I've been trying. Believe me."

Laura and I were soon outside looking for my car. The driver finally found us, and I approached the moment of truth. We drove to Laura's place, where my best friend also lives.

She asked, "Do you want to come up for a nightcap?"

"Do you want me to?"

"What the hell, sure. What's the worst that can happen?"

Well, I might rip your clothes off and have sex with you on the bed you share with Rob.

The doorman gave us a funny look. I began to think this wasn't a good idea. If one of these guys said something to Rob, Laura could be in deep shit. Or maybe, he wouldn't care. Or maybe, Rob would buy a gun and kill me and everybody else at Pyglet.

We arrived at her door and entered. It was beautifully furnished. She immediately kicked off her heels. "Why do women wear high heels? They're obviously uncomfortable, and they screw up your feet."

"We already discussed this. They make us more attractive. They optically lengthen our legs. But, you're right they hurt like hell by the end of an evening."

"You don't need to have your legs lengthened. They're beautiful."

"Thanks. I'll be right back. I want to slip into something more comfortable, to quote 1,000 movie actresses."

I sat down and turned on the television. It was time for "Seinfeld." I've seen every one of these episodes, but I still watch them over and over again. This one was about masturbation. Jerry, George, Kramer and Elaine bet each other that they could refrain from self-gratification. Great concept. I was laughing as Laura returned in a bathrobe.

"What are you laughing about? I heard you in my bedroom."

"Seinfeld, it's the masturbation skit."

"That's a very funny episode. So, do men masturbate often?"

"What a question. I guess it depends upon how horny a guy is and that depends upon how often he has sex."

She laughed. "I love the way you said that."

"Going out with the Palm sisters is not the worst thing in the world."

She laughed again. It was nice to see her smiling and happy. "I know, they never have headaches, and you don't have to kiss them good night."

"Actually, I do kiss them when we have a really good time." More laughing.

"I have a surprise for you, Stoke. I don't want you to get the wrong idea, but I think I should thank you for taking me out tonight."

"What is it? You shouldn't have."

Laura stood up and dropped her bathrobe. There she was in a tiny pushup bra and a black thong. She modeled for me, and I immediately had a woody. "So, what do you think?"

"You are the most beautiful woman on earth. Thongs were invented to be on your body."

She giggled. "I know you've been dreaming about this moment for a long time. You should savor it. At long last, you don't have to look at my thongs through my outer garments."

"Laura, thank you so much. This is the greatest moment of my whole life. It's a dream come true. I'm going to tell all the guys at work tomorrow that I actually saw 'the thong'."

"Don't you dare."

"Only kidding. But, would it be all right if I remembered this forever?"

"Sure. I'd be honored. It might come in handy the next time you date the Palm sisters."

"Now what, Laura?"

"Your call Stoke. Do you want to make love to me?"

"Yes. More than anything." I stood up and she approached me. She kissed me gently on the lips, and her tongue probed my mouth. Laura then reached down and fondled me. I was approaching the point of no return, and she knew it.

I said, "Laura, stop. I can't do this. Not now anyway. I can't disrespect Rob in this way."

"You're a good guy, Stoke." She pushed me onto the couch, reached behind and undid her bra and straddled me. She began to grind against me and pulled my head into her breasts. I started to kiss them and felt like I was going to explode.

"Really, we need to stop." I gently picked her up and set her down next to me. She covered her breasts in embarrassment.

"I want you to love me, Stoke. I need somebody to make me feel good. Don't you want me?"

"Believe me, I want to do it. It's just wrong. You need to work out your problems with Rob, one way or another."

As I walked home, I thought about what had just happened. I was a fool to walk away from this woman. She's the one I've desired for so long. But, was I in love, or was it just a fascination? I vowed not to get in a compromising situation until she worked out her problems.

Chapter 16

Amanda was forced to hang around with Best until every guest had departed. Then, Best spent several minutes with the Foundation people discussing the affair and how much money was raised.

What a horrible night. Amanda had to sit at the table dutifully as Best did her mistress of ceremonies routine. She felt like an accessory and knew full well that Best was using her. It was very fashionable in this business to have a same-sex relationship. At least, she was able to inform Stoke Spencer that she and Best weren't lovers.

All Amanda wanted to do was go home, get undressed and go to bed. Finally, Best approached her and said, "Okay darling, let's hit the road." They proceeded to the exit and Best then asked, "Did you have fun?"

"Not really. I was surprised at how few available straight men were present. Everyone had a date except me."

"I was your date. It's too bad you didn't have a better time. Chalk it up as a business meeting. But, I needed you by my side."

"Right." Amanda's response was noted by Best.

When they got into the car, Best said, "I really don't like your fucking attitude."

"Excuse me." Amanda was shocked by the way she spoke to her.

"You heard me." Best pushed a button, and the window between them and the driver went up. "Every event isn't going to be a party for you. I have responsibilities, and if I want you to accompany me, you will. You will act like your having a good time even if you aren't. Understood?"

"Yes ma'am." Amanda sensed this wasn't the right time or place for a confrontation.

They rode in silence and approached Best's building. She said, "Amanda, I'm sorry for being so hard on you. It was a long and difficult evening for both of us. In fact, I didn't even have one glass of champagne. Why don't you come up and have a nightcap with me."

Amanda thought it would be disastrous to say no. "Sure. I didn't have much to drink either."

When they arrived in Best's penthouse, Amanda was blown away. It was an outrageously beautiful place. What the heck, Best was a famous decorator. But the view of Central Park was breathtaking. "Your home is fabulous."

"Thanks. It took quite a while to find this unit and decorate it. Confidentially, it stretched me financially."

"Well, it was worth every penny."

"Did you speak with Stoke Spencer?"

"A little. He's nice, very opinionated and self assured."

Best made a strange face. "I think he's very unsure of himself with women."

"What do you mean?"

"His remarks to me were cutting, arrogant and downright hostile. Most men like him are successful in business, but in the bedroom, they're underachievers."

"Wow. That's quite an analysis."

"Honey, I've been around the block a few times, and I'll tell you right now, Stoke is no Alan Goldfarb behind between the sheets. Goldfarb's a stud."

"He should be. He probably had sex with every actress that ever worked for him."

"I'll bet he did. If you don't mind, I need to get out of this costume."

"No problem. I'll sit here and admire the view."

In a few minutes, Best returned in a silk bathrobe. Amanda saw that she had nothing on underneath the robe. Her antenna went up.

"How about some sparkly?"

"That would be great."

Best went to a beautiful mirrored bar, opened a refrigerator and drew out a bottle of Dom Perignon. "This should really hit the spot." She opened the bottle professionally without spilling a drop and filled two flute glasses. "Here you go." She sat down next to Amanda on the sofa.

Amanda touched glasses with Best and took a sip. It was heavenly. "Delicious."

"Glad you like it. So tell me, do you have any boyfriends?"

"No, but I'm looking for a man whenever I have spare time." Amanda noticed that Best's robe was open all the way up to her crotch.

"Can I ask you a personal question?"

"Sure." Amanda regretted that she had to answer in the affirmative.

"Have you ever been romantically involved with another woman?"

"That's a very personal question. I'm not sure I want to discuss my sexual preferences."

"Oh come on. Between us girls. Did you ever have sex with a woman?"

"When I was in college, I experimented with a lot of things. I smoked marijuana, and sexually, did some things that I'd just as soon forget."

"With men or women?"

"Let's just say I got involved in some testy situations."

"Well, I think you are beautiful, Amanda. You're also intelligent, well spoken, knowledgeable and creative. We can become a great team over time."

"Thank you. I appreciate your sentiments."

"But, we need to be, how shall I say it? We need to be soul mates and draw out the creative spirit in each other."

"What do you expect of me?"

Best moved closer and kissed Amanda on the lips. Much to Amanda's surprise, she didn't recoil. Was it because the kiss was gentle and affectionate? Or perhaps, Amanda's career was on the line, and so, she needed to be receptive. What was she prepared to do to further her ambition?"

Best backed off. "I think we should have a sensitive and deep relationship. Nothing exclusive or constraining. But, when either of us needs companionship, the other should be available."

"Okay."

Best moved closer again and kissed Amanda more sensually. She grabbed Amanda's hand and slid it under the robe and put it on her bare breast. Amanda instinctively caressed the magnificent, and remade, body part.

Then, Best pulled Amanda on top of her, and they began to grind against each other. Soon, Amanda took the lead. She refocused her attention on Best's legs and touched her most sensitive areas. Best began to moan and gave her greater access in response. The sexual tension was reaching a high level.

Suddenly, Amanda stopped and rose up. She was perspiring and was highly excited. But, she knew she was in dangerous territory. Best was accustomed to getting what she wanted, and Amanda just cut her off.

Also, Amanda's reaction to Best's advances was reflexive and not well considered. What was she feeling? It was totally different than being with a man. Was it forbidden fruit that tempted her? Was it because she was desperate for affection from a man, or woman? Or, was she making a career play- sex for success?

Amanda decided she better get this straight in her mind before it went too far. "Alex, I'm sorry. I'm very confused. I don't know if I'm really like this. I haven't had an intimate relationship for a long time, so it feels really great. But, I don't know what I want to do."

"You're so sweet. I understand. You should think about your needs and our relationship. The decisions you make will certainly have an impact on your career. I want to make love to you. You should know that."

"Thanks for understanding." Amanda wasn't sure whether Best was being kind or giving her an ultimatum. "I'm going to leave now. I'll see you at work in the morning."

Amanda walked home and thought about what had just transpired. She recognized her vulnerability, and it was wise to back off. But, being with another woman didn't turn her off. The real danger was mixing career and sex. She needed to tread carefully or her career at Best Design might be a short one.

Best continued to sip champagne and think about Amanda after she departed. The encounter was very stimulating, and Best opted for self gratification. The thought of Amanda in her grasp resulted in an explosive response. She was determined to have this young woman.

Chapter 17

The next day, I was really bummed out. My encounter with Laura ended unsatisfactorily. There she was, almost naked in her sexy thong. It was the vision I thought about a million times since I first met her. But, she was forbidden fruit, at least for the time being.

I asked myself how many friendships have been destroyed and wars fought when men and women fight for the attention of the opposite sex. Tens of millions, probably. Remember Helen of Troy, Jennifer and Brad and so many more.

I needed to speak with Rob to find out whether he was still in love with Laura. If he says his marriage is over, I suppose he wouldn't care if I courted Laura. But, would it play out that way?

Divorced men, even if they hate their ex-wives still get pissed when the woman they hate more than anyone else in the world is with another man. It's human nature. Men think they own their women forever. Women are like chattel in their minds.

I really didn't think I could concentrate on business when the love of my life was in such turmoil. Then, there was the developing opportunity with Alex Best. She really came on to me. Before anything happens with Laura, I should contact Alex to see if she's all show and no go.

Rob was returning from his business trip today, so maybe it would be wise to have another informal chat with him. Then, I saw Laura walk into the office

She was so beautiful. Her long blond hair fell below her shoulders. It was unencumbered just the way I like it. When Laura took off her coat, I noticed that she was wearing a short little black mini skirt. The ensemble was complete with a tight pink sweater that hugged her breasts. I'd bet anything she was wearing a thong under that skirt.

Laura saw me watching her, and she approached my office. Liz gave her a look when she passed her and said good morning.

I yelled out, "Laura, can I speak with you please?" I wanted to give her some cover. It's really difficult to hide anything in such a small environment like Pyglet.

"Sure Stoke."

"Come in. Please shut the door." I could feel Liz's evil stare. I was relieved when the door closed.

Laura spoke first, "About last night . . ."

"Please Laura, don't sweat it. Nothing happened. You were nice to accompany me to the dinner. That's all."

"You're so sweet to me, Stoke. I think I'm beginning to be really attracted to you."

"By the way, I haven't stopped envisioning you in your thong. Are you wearing one today?"

"Yes. Do you want to see it?" She started to hike up her skirt.

"Stop it, please. Behave yourself. Somebody might walk in on us, like your husband. Or worse, Liz might interrupt us like she did that other time."

"Liz would definitely be much worse than Rob." She laughed.

"So, what's going to happen next?" I asked.

"What do you mean?"

"Well, what about your relationship with Rob?"

"I told you, it's over."

"Does he know that?"

"It's his wish."

"Did he say that to you?"

"Stoke, women know when a relationship is over. Most won't admit it, but we all know."

"Are you sad?"

"Sure I am. We had a great love affair, but Rob can't be tied down. It's not his nature to be constrained in any way."

"He's like that in business too. The only reason why he stays at Pyglet is because he has free rein. Do you think you will divorce?"

"I suppose so. We need to have a confrontation, and hopefully, agree that we need to go our separate ways."

"Should I speak with Rob?"

"About what?"

"Come on Laura. You know, all this stuff."

"I don't care one way or the other."

"I can't be disloyal to Rob. We can't be together until you settle all matters with him."

"That makes sense. I think it would be unwise to start cheating on him now although I'm tempted by your charms."

I wondered about the last comment based upon the events of the previous evening. "Then, it's settled. I have to receive a green light from both of you before we hook up."

"Just one qualification. I don't need Rob's approval to do anything. We are finished. As far as I'm concerned, I'm a free agent."

"I understand all that, but I do need his concurrence to save my friendship and my company."

"Okay. I better get to work. Are you sure you don't want to see my ass before I leave?"

"All right, you talked me into it." She pulled her skirt up to her waist and there it was, a tiny pink thong.

"Bye Stoke." She smoothed out her skirt and walked out.

In a nanosecond, Liz was in my office and the door was closed. "What the fuck is going on? Are you involved with her again?"

"Nothing's going on, yet."

"What the hell does that mean? Are you planning to molest her and be sued again, or worse, beaten to death by her husband?"

"Relax. I'm smarter than you give me credit for."

"Bullshit. Your brain is lodged in the head of your dick."

"Would you please calm down?"

"Rob is your best friend and your partner. Why would you covet his wife? Are you losing your mind?"

"I'm not doing anything until they formally split."

"What do you mean? Are they breaking up?"

"Yes."

"Who said so?"

"Laura."

"What did Rob say about all this?"

"I haven't spoken with him yet."

"Well, you better slow down until you do. You don't want to be in the middle of a shit storm."

"I agree. Last night Laura came on to me, and I walked away."

"You're so full of it. You're not strong enough to turn her down. You've been after her tight little ass for years."

"Well, I did. I said I wouldn't sleep with her until she broke up with Rob."

"I hope you know what you're doing."

"And don't talk to Laura about any of this."

"I won't unless she brings it up or sues you again for harassment." Liz stormed out. It was shaping up to be a pretty interesting day. Maybe, I'll do some business before the day is done.

A few minutes passed, and Rob came strolling through the door. He deposited his briefcase and overnight bag in his office and made a beeline to my area. He didn't even make a detour to say hello to his wife. Weird.

"Ah, the merry wanderer. Did you make any money for me today?"

"Maybe, that's why I came to see you. The W Pictures deal is ours. All you need to do is stroke Alan Goldfarb, and we're off to the races."

"How should I do that?"

"He's having a party at his new house in the Hamptons on Saturday. We're invited. The place will be overflowing with porn stars. Even you'll be able to get laid at the affair."

"Don't be a wise ass. I have plans this weekend." I really didn't.

"Cancel them. You're coming with me, and we're going to a party."

"What about Laura?"

"What about her?"

"Is she going with us?"

"What the hell for? You think she'd be comfortable with the people that'll be at Goldfarb's house?"

"We need to talk about you and Laura. What's going on?"

"I told you. We're going to wind down."

"You're not serious."

"I am. I can't be with her anymore. I'm suffocating. By the way, how was your date with her last night?"

"It wasn't a real date. I needed someone to accompany me to a rubber chicken dinner."

"Did you knock off a piece?"

"You mean did your wife and I sleep together?"

"Yeah. Did you?"

"Don't you care?"

"No. I got laid in Cleveland last night. It's the first time I cheated on Laura since we got married. It was sensational. If I can fool around, so can she."

"I don't understand you. Laura is a fantastic woman. She's beautiful, intelligent, everything a man could want."

"I don't want to be married to her any longer."

"I see."

"Are you going to ask Laura on a real date? You should."

"I don't know. It would be so uncomfortable, don't you think?"

"I have no problem with it. Do what you want. In fact, if you go out with Laura, I'll feel less guilty."

"So, you're going to get divorced?"

"Yes. I will discuss it with her tonight. Come on Stoke, you've been drooling over my wife for years. Here's your big opportunity."

"And you don't think it would be bizarre?"

"No, Stoke, I don't care."

"I don't know what to say. What will everybody at Pyglet think?"

"Who cares? You're the largest owner of the company, and I'm the next largest."

"You don't think this will affect our working relationship?"

"Why should it? I want out. She wants out. And, you want her. Simple equation."

"Okay. I'll think about it. And, I can't wait to see what Mr. Goldfarb has in store for his guests. How much can we make from our deal with him? What is the deal, by the way?"

"W Pictures will borrow two hundred and fifty million dollars and pay it as a dividend to Goldfarb. The company's net worth is at least five hundred million. It has no debt and earns about sixty million dollars before depreciation and taxes. We should earn 3% on the debt placement, at least seven and a half million dollars, plus a five million dollar advisory fee. How's that?"

"Super. This guy's clean, right?"

"He's probably a pervert, but all of his female employees fuck for a living, so it's a perfect match."

"You better make sure this guy doesn't have any skeletons in his closet. I mean it, Rob. If his sex life comes back to haunt us, I'll have your ass."

"Will do." I'm out of here. I'm going to take Laura home right now, tell her I want a divorce and move into a hotel."

"Good luck. I'm sorry this is happening, Rob.

"No problem. I feel liberated."

I felt terrible about Laura and Rob. What a great couple they were. Oh well, it just wasn't meant to be.

I yelled out to Liz, "Can you get Alexandra Best of Best Design on the phone?"

"Are you going to give me any clues about how to reach this woman?"

"Give me a break. Her company is in New York. She's a famous designer. Just get her."

"Yes massa."

I thought, "bitch."

About five minutes later Liz intercommed me, "Ms. Best on the line for you."

"Shut the door, Liz."

"Hello Alex, how are you?"

"I'm fine Stoke and very glad to hear from you. I will speak with you only if you're asking me out and/or increasing your pledge to the Foundation."

"Still very pushy. I'll take door number one. How do you look on Friday?"

"I'm busy, but I'll cancel for you. And, I always look good."

"What's your pleasure?"

She said, "I want a late dinner, and then I want to dance, dirty dance."

"How about Nobu?"

"Great. I'll take you to my favorite dance club after we eat."

"It's a date." I hung up and thought that Friday looked promising.

Chapter 18

The next day, Jake Sardi called Best.

"Ms. Best's office."

"Tell her Jake is on the line."

"Will do."

"What's up Jake?"

"How are you coming along with the new client?"

"Very well. I'm going out to his new place in the Hamptons for a party on Saturday."

"Who is this guy?"

"Name's Alan Goldfarb."

"What's his business?"

"He's in the soft core porn business?"

"Get the fuck outta here. You've stooped to a new low, Alex. You'd do anything to make a buck."

"He's loaded. I understand porno is a money machine these days. Personally, I'm not into it."

"Well I am. Why wasn't I invited?"

"Because you're a dirt bag."

"Watch your mouth."

"What's going on with Tom Gordon?" Alex asked.

"Some of my buddies scared the shit out of him the other day. I haven't heard anything new."

"Well, maybe you ought to follow up. I don't want the cops knocking on my door."

"Relax, the guy's a pussy."

. . .

At that very moment, Tom Gordon was meeting with Richard Head, Assistant District Attorney.

After a few minutes of chit chat, Head asked, "So tell me about your situation, Mr. Gordon. The police said you've been defrauded by a house decorator and assaulted by a man she works with."

"That's right, Mr. Head. I bought a new home about a year ago and Alex Best, she's the decorator, redid the place."

"Was it expensive?"

"Terribly so. I spent two million and a half dollars."

"Wow, it must be quite a place."

"Yeah, it is. But I probably overpaid by at least five hundred grand."

"And you were assaulted?"

"Yes. After I threatened to go to the police, a guy named Jake Sardi, Best's furniture supplier, had some of his New York punks attack me."

"Were you hurt seriously?"

"Messed up my face and gave me very sore ribs. But nothing permanent."

"Tell me more about the relationship between Sardi and Best."

"Sardi manufactures furniture for Best's clients in North Carolina. They screwed me by padding the bills."

"Aren't you frightened they'll attack you again if they find out we spoke."

"Of course. But you can protect me, right?"

"Sure, we'll take care of you."

"What are you going to do now?"

"I'm going to investigate, so they will soon know that someone reported them to the authorities."

"And how will I be protected?"

"We'll put some cops outside your home until this affair comes to a conclusion."

"Do I need to do anything else?"

"Yes. I'll need to see a record of all your dealings with Best and Sardi."

"I want you to rake these people over the coals. They stole from me, and they hurt me physically."

"Don't worry, Mr. Gordon, I'll put them behind bars if I can prove they did these things. Is there anything else you want to tell me that might be helpful in an investigation?"

Gordon thought maybe he should tell Head about his fling with Best but decided not to. "No."

"I'll be in touch." The meeting ended.

. . .

Rob strolled into my office and clearly had something on his mind. I wondered whether he was going to give me details about his conversation with Laura last night.

"What are you thinking about? Your marriage?"

"Hell no. It's over, Stoke. Laura is yours if you want her."

"Thanks." That was pretty easy. I guess I've been cleared to court Laura.

"I told her I wanted out, and she said she did too. Not a very long chat at all."

"Are you getting a lawyer?"

"Yeah, we're going to use the same person. There's nothing contentious here. We'll divide up the property, agree on some alimony for a few years, and that's it."

"Your marriage has been distilled into just those few words? You have no regrets?"

"Nope. Laura is a beautiful, sexy woman. We had a lot of fun, but it's time to move on."

"What about Pyglet?"

"What do you mean?"

"Can you two work together?"

"Sure, we can be civil. No big deal."

"Does Laura feel the same way?"

"I think so. You should ask her about all this before you try to date her." He smiled at me.

I can't believe Rob knows I want to get his wife in bed, and he doesn't care. He really is the exception to the rule. Most men feel contempt for their ex-wives and their boyfriends. Not Rob. He doesn't give a damn. "So, you really wouldn't care if I asked Laura on a date."

"I think I answered that question twenty times already. No, Stoke, no. It's okay. I'm a mature person. I'm going to bang my brains out with other women. Do what ever you want. I'll even tell you all about Laura, what turns her on, what sexual positions she prefers, whatever." He laughed.

"That's not funny, Rob. And, I don't need any advice from you."

"Can we change the subject?"

"Sure. You want to discuss W Pictures?"

"Yes. I know a senior guy at American Bank. He's been busting my chops to bring him some business and can easily bridge the entire loan. Then we can syndicate long-term debt to some insurance companies to take him out. By doing it this way, we close out all possible competition for the business."

"Nice plan."

"There's one other thing. My buddy is a real horn dog. He loves chasing pussy. He and I did some tom-catting before I was married. I think we should ask him to join us out in the Hamptons. If he gets laid, it'll make the whole process go much smoother."

"That's fine with me. I hope I get laid too. Can this guy's bank buy the whole deal?"

"I already said he could. He's a senior person at the bank."

"Okay. Ask him if he wants to go on a road trip. Tell him to bring protection." We both laughed.

Rob exited and proceeded to his office. On the way, he passed Laura's area.

"How are you?"

"Not so great," she responded. "And you?"

"I'm fine. You want to chat for a minute."

"Okay. I'll come to your office." Stoke noticed the encounter from his vantage point.

After she arrived, Laura sat on the couch in Rob's office. "What do you want to talk about?" Rob queried.

"Well, we covered a lot of ground last night. I thought you might want to reflect on some of the things we discussed. I feel terrible that our relationship is ending. I can't believe we were so in love, and now it means nothing."

"Look, we had a great time together. I loved being with you. I really did. But, I've changed. My needs are different now."

"That's a lot of bullshit, Rob. You just want to get back into the action. You miss fucking around with different women. You're a narcissistic asshole."

"Whoa. Slow down. It takes two to tango. Maybe it's you who should take responsibility for what's happened."

"I would if I knew what I did wrong. One second we're happy, making love, going out and then you lose interest in me. It's not a great feeling to be a woman whose man is never at home."

"I work hard. That's no crime."

"Even when you were with me, you were distant, always thinking of other things."

"I don't know what to say except I'm sorry."

"For what? Ruining my life?"

"Oh, I'll bet you recover very quickly. Stoke can't wait to get his hands on you, if you haven't already slept with him."

"Fuck you." Laura walked out and slammed the door. Everybody looked up, and then went back to their business.

Stoke dialed Laura's number. "It's me. Are you okay?"

"No. I feel like shit."

"You want to have lunch with me?"

"I'm not up to it. But, I'll take a rain check."

I had a feeling that this whole affair was going to be very disruptive in a number of ways. How the hell is this office supposed to work efficiently while two important members are at war with each other? And, to assume they will get along through the divorce process was naïve. Also, what if I date Laura? The first time I have sex with her I won't be able to stop smiling all day. Everybody will know that I finally de-thonged her. Very funny, Stoke?

Chapter 19

After Laura went back to her desk, Rob phoned Donny Cohen at American Bank.

"Mr. Cohen's office."

"It's Rob Viand calling for him, please."

"Hold on."

"Rob, how's it hangin' brother? It's been a while. How's your beautiful wife?"

"Actually, Laura and I just broke up. I'm a free man again."

"Are you cool with the breakup?"

"Very. I guess I'm not the marrying type."

"Neither am I. I suppose you're looking for someone to go whoring with."

"That and one other thing. Stoke Spencer and I are working on a deal with a company called W Pictures. We need a bridge loan for the company. Thought you might be interested."

"What kind of pictures does the company make?"

"Soft core porn."

"You're shitting me."

"It's not the rude stuff. Simulated sex. Titillating shit that's on late night cable."

"How much you lookin' for?"

"Two hundred fifty to be taken out with a debt placement that Pyglet will place. Owner wants to pay a big dividend to himself. The company's worth about 500 million and has no debt. Very profitable."

"Well, American doesn't do much porno business. But, if I don't syndicate the loan, and it's outstanding for less than six months, we wouldn't have a public relations issue."

"That's the plan. You get a big upfront fee and a high rate of interest while the loan's outstanding."

"I'm interested. What's the next step?"

"I'll send you some financials that you can mull over. And more importantly, the owner is having an orgy at his new place in the Hamptons on Saturday. The party will be chock full of actresses. You're invited. Stoke told me to tell you to bring protection." They both laughed.

"Wow. Sounds terrific. Count me in."

"My assistant will call yours with the details. We leave late morning on Saturday. Remember to bring your thong along with the rubbers."

"All right. See ya."

The week was finally coming to an end. I tried, unsuccessfully, to get Laura to meet me outside of the office. She said no each time I asked indicating that she needed more time to think.

That was okay with me as I had a date with Alex Best, and then, Rob, his banker pal and I were heading to the Hamptons for a day of debauchery.

Liz made a reservation for this evening at Nobu uptown at nine, and Alex was supposed to take care of the club arrangements. I hired a car to transport us for the entire evening.

Chapter 20

I arrived at Alex's apartment on Central Park West at 8:30. I went into the lobby and told the doorman I was there to see Ms. Best. Naked, preferably.

"Ms. Best left word for you to go directly up to her place on the 12th floor. It's the only apartment on the landing."

"Thanks." I trundled to the elevator bank and waited for the car to open. I looked at a mirror to assess my outfit. I wore black linen jeans, a charcoal grey sport coat and a highly starched white dress shirt. I thought I looked pretty sharp for an old guy.

I exited the elevator and stood in her foyer. Suddenly, Alex appeared and approached me.

"Nice to see you Stoke." She gave me a peck on the cheek. I examined her as she walked ahead into the living room. Do women know that every time men walked behind them, we check out their asses?

She had on a black, micro mini leather skirt that was just the right length, very short. Her legs were buff and amazing for a 30-something year old cougar. I mean really nice. The skirt was skintight and hugged her gorgeous rump. On top, she had a loose fitting purple silk blouse. I love the way silk hangs off of big knockers. I was aroused, and I hadn't even said ten words to the woman.

"Care for a drink."

"Absolutely. How about some scotch on the rocks?"

"Make it yourself. The bar is right behind you."

I didn't notice the bar because I was staring at her ass. Soon, I was comfortable in an easy chair with drink in hand. Alex sat across from me. She wasn't shy about showing off her legs when she reclined, and I wasn't shy about looking at them.

"Well, what did you think about the Foundation gala?"

"Pretty much like most events I attend. You raised a lot of money, so congratulations for that."

"The Foundation people were ecstatic about the pledges we received. I paraded around all evening begging for money."

"You looked great. And, you look spectacular tonight." I wouldn't mind sitting here all night ogling your body.

"Why thank you."

"So, you decorate homes."

"I do. My company is very successful. We service large apartments in the city and estates out on Long Island, mostly in the Hamptons."

"You must meet some interesting characters."

"Well, our services are super expensive. You get what you pay for. So, most of my clients are wealthy."

"Do you often have repeat business?"

"That's the principal test of success. If I can get someone to pay me a stupid amount of money a second time, I'm doing my job well." We giggled.

"My business is similar. Clients pay me for my brainpower."

"So, what exactly do you do? I don't know a thing about banking."

"Companies buy and sell assets, and we orchestrate the transactions. Others need money to make acquisitions. We arrange loans. Pretty mundane stuff. The good news is that our fees are astronomical, stupid, just like yours."

"You make a lot of money?"

"Yup. In fact, Mr. Obama thinks I make too much. But what the hell does he know? Are you ready for dinner? I hope you like sushi."

"Love it."

We left her building, got into the car and made the short trip to the restaurant. Nobu is a pretentious, crazy-priced Japanese eatery. Getting reservations is a real challenge. But, the food is really outstanding, and the service is superb. I love going there even though I feel like I've been robbed every time I do.

It was balmy outside so Alex wore a shawl over her shoulders. We bypassed the coat check and were directed to the hostess on the second floor. "Hello Mr. Spencer. Nice to see you again."

Alex commented, "I gather you're a regular?"

"What can I say? I love the smell of fish." She gave me a funny look.

We were taken to a power table, near the entrance to the dining room so everyone would see us as they entered. I bet Alex's skirt was way up high on her legs. She seemed like the kind of woman that tried to bait men for sport, a real cockteaser.

Alex ordered one of those fancy cosmopolitan concoctions, a real sissy drink. It drove me crazy to see men embarrass themselves when they ordered drinks with liqueurs and umbrellas in them. I asked for a scotch, Johnnie Walker Blue. They charge about fifty bucks for a shot of Blue, but I don't care.

We spoke about our backgrounds. Alex told me that she was an only child brought up in Manhattan. She attended one of the prominent girl schools on the Upper East Side and then went to Columbia.

"Did you enjoy Columbia?" Stupid question, but I needed to recognize the lady's academic credentials.

"It was great. I knew where to go to party when I wasn't studying. I was a history major, which I loved."

"How did you get into the decorating business?"

"I worked as an intern at a few designer companies while attending college. One of them offered me a job. I'm a terrific artist, and I have wonderful taste if I say so myself." She smiled.

Alex's phone rang, and she answered it. I sat there like a jerk until she hung up. I hate when people use cell phones at dinner. Good restaurants should require that their clientele check phones at the door along with their coats and concealed weapons.

"Sorry about that. Big deal."

"No offense, but I think it's rude to speak on a cell at dinner while your tablemate sits and waits."

"I said I was sorry. What the hell's your problem?"

"I just told you. I don't like waiting around for people to finish their calls. We're out together. Let's enjoy it, or I can just bring you home now."

"Jeez. You're really vicious when something irks you."

"Let's make a deal. I won't answer my phone if you don't answer yours. How about it?"

"Okay, I'm game. I never thought I would agree to not use my cell under any circumstances. But, I'm willing to make an investment in your case." She grinned evilly.

We discussed our respective businesses, our former marriages and all that sort of crap.

All of a sudden, a very effeminate and overweight man approached us and screamed, "Hello beautiful Alexandra."

She responded, "How are you Archibald?"

I thought, Archibald? Is this guy kidding? The big slob was dressed in a robe, probably because he couldn't find normal clothes that fit him. He reached over and kissed Alex on the mouth, on her cheeks and on her hands. The only thing he didn't kiss was her ass. I was hoping to do that later in the evening.

"You never call me. You never give me any business. Can I sit with you?" He sat down before I had a chance to say no.

"Archibald, this my friend Stoke. Stoke, Archibald."

"Charmed," I said. He ignored me and continued falling all over Alex, who seemed to be enjoying all the adulation.

After a few minutes of Archibald's slobbering, I spoke up, "Archie, what do you do?"

"My name is Archibald, my friend. And, I'm afraid it might be too complicated for you to understand."

"Are you creative, an artiste?"

"As a matter of fact, I am."

"Well, I'm a creative person myself."

"That's hard to believe. Look at the way you're dressed." He turned back to Alex and smirked.

"Look who's talking? You're a big fat shit. You think that tent you're wearing is fashionable? Why don't you get the fuck out of here? Alex and I are tying to have dinner. You're so gross that I'm starting to lose my appetite. And, I'm sure you couldn't afford a meal here. I'm certainly not going to pay for you."

"Alex, where did you find this disgusting man?"

"I think you had better leave, Archibald. I'll call you."

As he got up, I flashed my middle finger at him and mouthed the words affiliated to the gesture."

"Stoke, you weren't very nice to my friend. You're so aggressive."

"Do you like aggressive men?"

"Yes, but mostly in bed."

"Well, you'll have to wait until later for that."

The food came and it was delicious. We were drinking still water along with white wine. At one point, a waiter started filling Alex's Chardonnay glass with water.

She went berserk, "What the fuck are you doing, you idiot?" The waiter was a young Asian man. He was mortified by Alex's verbal assault.

"Did I do something wrong madam?"

"Yes, you poured water into my wine. Don't you know the difference between water and wine?"

"Of course I do. I will get you another glass."

"We're spending a fortune for this meal, and you're mixing different drinks together. Are you stupid?" Actually, I was the one spending a fortune.

Suddenly, the headwaiter intervened and asked if there was a problem. In a very loud voice, Alex expressed her displeasure yet again. He apologized and gave us a new bottle of wine.

"Make sure we get someone else to wait on our table."

"Yes madam." He gave her a "stick it up your ass" look.

"Wow," I said. "We make quite a couple, like two kegs of dynamite ready to explode."

Some man at another table was staring at us during the wine episode. I couldn't determine whether he was watching Alex do her nasty act or whether he was ogling her, not that I blame him.

I said, "Something I can do for you?"

"You talking to me," he responded like Tony Soprano. He was a big lug, who looked like he ate more than his fair share of pasta and meatballs when he wasn't sucking down sushi.

"Yes, keep your eyes off of us."

"I was just watching your bitch perform. Very impressive. She must be hot in the sack with that attitude and her great ass. I think she might need a beating, though."

"You better mind your manners, punk. Be a gentleman."

"I would if the bitch was a lady."

His buddies were hysterical laughing at this point, which only served to infuriate me. I got up and walked over the wise guy. "Why don't you keep your fucking nose out of our business, smart ass?"

The buddies said, "Whoa" and "Watch out Gino this guy's gonna kick your butt."

"What are you going to do about it, you old prick?"

I picked up a glass of water and threw it into his face. He jumped up but was intercepted by the bouncers who had been monitoring the action.

I said, "Alex, let's get out of here." I threw five one hundred dollar bills on our table as the irate goon screamed profanities at me.

"That was really fun, Stoke," Alex said to me outside the restaurant. "Thanks for coming to my rescue. I'll have to give you a reward later." She winked at me.

By this time, nailing Alex was a foregone conclusion. I needed to insure that I didn't drink too much, lest my sexual performance be deemed substandard. And, I probably shouldn't throw drinks into any other people's faces, especially Mafia-type wise guys.

"So, where next? You said you knew of a hot place to go dancing. I have all this energy to work off. I'm ready to burn up the dance floor." Alex gave directions to the driver, someplace in the Village.

We pulled up to a warehouse with no sign. Two large, and mean-looking African-American monsters protected the entrance.

Alex led the way and said, "Hi big boys."

One of the two ape-men smiled and said, "Hello Ms. Best. How are you tonight?"

"I'm great. How's the action?"

"You're a little early." It was nearly midnight. "But the crowd's getting revved up, and the music's smoking."

"Good. I like it that way."

"Ms. Best, you're smoking this evening."

"Why thank you Maurice. If my friend, Mr. Spencer, gets into any trouble, would you please watch over him?"

"No problem."

I figured I had to pay for the insurance so I slipped Maurice a Benjamin. "Thank you, Mr. Spencer. You are covered." Maurice said something to his evil twin, who led us inside.

Well, the place was really wild. Very attractive environment, half nude dancers were gyrating on the floor to the DJ's tunes. If the music was any louder, it might have made me permanently deaf.

"Want a drink?" I asked Alex.

"No, I have something better," at which time she pulled out a small vial filled with white powder from the tiny purse that hung around her neck. Alex sprinkled some dust on her finger and snorted it.

"Have at hit."

"No thanks. I already have a drinking problem. I don't need another addiction."

Immediately, I could sense the change in Alex's demeanor. She dragged me onto the floor and began to slink around erotically and rub me in a very suggestive way. She stuck her ass out and grinded it against my groin.

I grabbed her and started to slow dance even though the music called for a fast dance of some sort. Alex took the opportunity to push her pelvis into mine. You know what I did? I grabbed both of her butt cheeks and pushed against her. They were very fine cheeks, I might add.

At the point of sheer exhaustion, we took a break and I ordered some drinks. We found a nook in the room where I could almost hear Alex speaking.

"So, how do you like the club?" She asked me as she took another hit of the white powder. I respectfully declined and drank my gin on the rocks.

"The place is great. There are a ton of beautiful women. Although you are the hottest of the lot."

"You're a real lady's man, aren't you Stoke?"

"I do my best." She moved closer and kissed me hard. Her tongue probed my mouth, and I sucked it.

"I'm really turned on."

"I'm pretty excited myself."

She knelt down, unzipped my fly and pulled out my penis. I said, "Alex, what the hell are you doing? This isn't the ideal place for oral sex."

"Don't you want a blowjob?"

"Of course I do. But, I'd rather you do it in private."

She stood up, and I zipped up. She said, "Let's dance."

We moved to the floor, and I bumped into a very exuberant male dancer, who almost knocked me off my feet.

Fred Astaire said, "What the fuck?" That's probably not what the real Fred would say in a similar circumstance.

I said, "Watch what your doing, sunny boy."

"Hey grandpa, how about I punch your fucking lights out?"

Here we go again. "Fuck you, punk" was my retort. We were officially in a fuck you contest.

Alex reached across and scratched the man's face. He made a move at Alex, and suddenly Maurice and his partner punched the would-be stud a couple of time in the gut and dragged him away. The guy's dance partner just turned around and started grooving with someone else.

"I guess Maurice really meant it. I'm covered tonight."

"My boys will look out for us. You're in the safest place in Manhattan, Stoke."

"I'll just slap anybody who pisses me off. Is that okay? Will your bodyguards take care of me?"

"Absolutely. Slap away." We laughed, and danced and laughed.

I was starting to run out of gas and said to Alex, "Let's get going. I'm not used to this early morning gig."

"Sure."

We exited. I said thanks to Maurice and gave him a C-note for saving my life from the maniac in the club. "Thanks for bailing me out."

"No problem, Mr. Spencer. You come here whenever. We'll make sure you have a good time." I gave them a cool guy's handshake, and we jumped in my car.

I told the driver to bring us back to Alex's place. Meanwhile, Alex took another hit of her fairy dust. I wondered whether the white stuff increased her sexual drive.

We arrived, and I just followed Alex to her apartment. I didn't even ask if I could come up.

As soon as I closed the door, Alex's was all over me, kissing, licking and saying dirty words. It was exhilarating. My prospects, along with one of my body parts, were growing.

"I want to kiss you. I want to make love right now." She said in a very sexy voice.

"Well okay."

Alex pulled my pants down in her foyer and accosted my manhood once again. I was only slightly more comfortable, as my pants and boxers were around my ankles, and I was in a hallway. This woman was not going to be denied the chance to go down on me. Who am I to complain? So, I just stood there and let Alex do her thing.

After a few minutes of sucking and slurping, she got up and said, "Follow me."

I shuffled along after her like a puppy dog. As we entered her workshop, otherwise known as her bedroom, she was stripping off articles of clothing. By the time she got to the bed, she was down to her bra and panties. What a fantastic body.

"Take off your clothes," she ordered, and I complied. "Lay down on the bed." I did. She continued what she started in the foyer except now I was comfortably on my back. Then, the vial appeared again, and she snorted more of the nose candy. The drug caused her to increase the tempo of the task in hand, so to speak.

"I want you to kiss me now." I was her slave. Worst things could happen to guy. She rose up and took off her remaining two pieces of clothes and lay spread-eagled on her back. "Kiss my breasts hard." I buried my face into them. "Bite them." It was starting to get a little too kinky, but I was too pumped up not comply, so I followed her orders.

Then Alex grabbed my hair and guided me below her waist. She forced my head into her crotch. In less than thirty seconds she was shaking like a California earthquake.

Alex thrust up, and I went flying onto to my back. She soon followed and mounted me like an Arabian. For the next few moments, it was a relentless hump and grind absent any tenderness or emotion. Soon she was undulating at warp speed. She screamed, shuddered and fell off of me.

I attempted to get on top of her, but she pushed me away and was soon sound asleep. What the hell just happened to me? I felt like I was raped. It was an impersonal sexual act. And worse yet, it resulted in no gratification for me. It was all Alex.

In a few moments, she began to snore. Then it came to me. This experience was like the scene in the movie *Network* when Faye Dunaway had sex with William Holden. Dunaway was on top and had an orgasm in just seconds like an inconsiderate man. Holden was just as unsatisfied in the movie as I was now.

It was four a.m., and I needed to get to get some sleep for the field trip to Goldfarb's party. Maybe, I'll have a more fulfilling encounter tomorrow.

CHAPTER 21

My alarm went off at nine. I felt like shit after a really late night with Alex Best. It was a weird experience for sure.

Best is a gorgeous physical specimen, but she's also a domineering wench, who needs to be in control of every aspect of her life. Even while involved in the throes of passion, she had to give all the orders. And, her gratification was paramount. I was no more than a human vibrator as far as she was concerned.

There was no upside for me to continue an intimate relationship with Best. Based upon her attitude last night, I wouldn't be surprised if the woman was involved in all sorts of unsavory activities, cocaine use being one of them.

The doorman buzzed me at ten to tell me that Rob was waiting for me. Eating dinner late, dancing, drinking and fucking until the wee hours of the morning were the principal causes of my splitting headache and nausea. I almost called Rob to tell him I couldn't make the trip. But, a lot of money was at stake. If Goldfarb hired Pyglet to do his deal, my company stood to earn millions. And besides, the party was supposed to be populated with a gaggle of porno actresses available to please us. How could I miss it?

When I exited the building, Rob and Donny Cohen, from American Bank, were sitting in Rob's 750 BMW laughing loudly. "What the hell's so funny?" I asked.

Rob responded, "Did you have a tough night with Ms. Best?"

"Don't even go there. I just got home a few hours ago."

"Stoke, you remember Donny Cohen."

"How are you, Donny? Are you ready to get into some trouble?"

"I'm always ready for trouble if it involves hot women. Rob tells me the party is going to be chock full of porno sluts. Never had the pleasure."

Rob jumped in, "Well, hang on to your hat. Goldfarb aims to please."

The trip to the Hamptons seemed endless. I felt like vomiting the entire way. No way, I could doze with Donny in the car. He asked a thousand questions about W Pictures and Goldfarb's reputation. The latter was beginning to concern me more and more.

Rob answered most of the questions, so it was an opportunity for me to learn more about Goldfarb and the proposed transaction as well.

Cohen was adamant that the proposed bridge loan be very short term and zeroed in on Pyglet's ability to sell bonds to repay the loan. I assured him that, based upon W Pictures financials, Rob and I could sell the bonds. I had some questions in my own mind about investor interest in financing a pornographer, but if we priced it generously, it shouldn't be a problem. We can offer investors a "fornication" premium.

At long last, the trip came to an end. It took longer to get to Goldfarb's place in the Hamptons because the traffic was horrific after we passed through Southampton. At that point, thousands of cars converge onto a two-lane road for the last several miles to Bridgehampton. The only benefit was that it was a beautiful, sunny day and all the Hamptons trophy wives were out in force sashaying around town. From the car, we saw many delightful female specimens, which we admired along the way. I was starting to get revved up for the Goldfarb soiree.

We drove up to the pornographer's estate and were taken aback by his monstrous house and expansive property, which was located on the beach. The party was already in high gear as scores of women walked around in micro bikinis and thongs. I never saw so many fabulous asses in one place. Unfortunately, many of the men were similarly exposed.

The three of us walked into Goldfarb's backyard after Rob handed his car keys to a valet. We were dressed in walking shorts and polo shirts more appropriate for a day on the golf links. I brought a bathing suit with me, which, to be honest, was way to dorky for this crowd. But, I wasn't inclined to expose my fat ass in a thong, and I didn't own one in any case.

Rob winked at me as a group of gals made their way past us and smiled. Things were looking up. I could see Donny's mouth watering and whispered to him, "I hope you have your Trojans."

Donny said, "Screw the protection, I'm going bareback today." We laughed.

Suddenly, Goldfarb appeared, all six foot two inches of him. He wore Speedo swim trunks and looked amazing for a man of his age. His gray hair was distinguished, but he had the body of a thirty year-old who worked out every day. Two sweet things were hanging all over Goldfarb. Some women would do anything to get their faces on the silver screen.

"Welcome, gentlemen."

I replied, "Nice to be here, Alan. Thanks for the invite. I love your friends. They're all so . . . great to look at."

"I'm positive you'll see more of them as the party progresses."

"I can't wait. Of course, you know Rob, and this is our good friend Donny Cohen from American Bank. He's interested in learning the naked truth about W Pictures."

"Good to meet you, Alan. I heard plenty about W Pictures and about your ass . . . ets."

"Very funny, Donny. I need to remember that one."

Goldfarb offered to give us a quick tour of the property and his home, which was currently unfurnished, later in the day. He said he wanted to have a party before he spent a fortune decorating it. I totally understood his perspective. I wouldn't want DNA sprayed all over my new furniture either.

"I assume you're going to use a big time decorator to fix up the place." I chimed in.

"Absolutely, I hired a woman named Alex Best to decorate my humble abode."

Rob looked at me and snickered. I said, "Alex is a friend of mine." Rob snickered again.

"Oh, has she worked on you?" He grinned.

"Actually she has, but it didn't involve furniture." I said. "We first met last week at a charity affair, and, as a matter of fact, we had dinner last night." I left out the part about humping like dogs in heat.

"Is that so?"

"I understand she is the best at what she does."

"That's what I heard too. In fact, Alex is right over there with her colleague Amanda Lane."

I looked over my shoulder, and there she was. We smiled and waved at each other. I couldn't believe the bitch was here and would likely try to ruin my afternoon.

Goldfarb excused himself and headed towards some men who definitely weren't porno actors. I could tell because they had middle-aged bellies and were dressed in dorky walking shorts just like us. Maybe they were investors.

Alex and Amanda approached, and I broke away from Rob and Donny. There was no need to introduce them.

I said, "Well, we meet again. Seems like we are involved with the same crowd."

"Hi Stoke. You remember Amanda?"

"Of course I do. How are you, Amanda?"

"I'm fine thanks. She didn't look very happy about being at the party. The poor girl was being dragged about by her boss.

I looked Best over. She was wearing a short summer dress with a pastel print. The woman had a dynamite body. I regretted that my experience with her wasn't more rewarding. She never gave me a chance to fully enjoy all of her wonders. Actually, she just didn't give a shit about my needs.

"Amanda, Stoke and I went out on the town last night. We had a great time."

"Yeah, it was really fun." I forced myself to lie. "Alex and I got into a couple of tiffs during the evening, one in Nobu and one at her dance club."

"Stoke saved me from a ruffian at the restaurant," Alex chimed in.

"Right. I had to threaten the brute with a beating, and he cowered." That was a total lie, of course. Alex and I laughed.

"Amanda, will you excuse us for a moment? I'd like to have a private word with Stoke."

"Sure, I'll circulate a bit. Maybe I'll meet a porno stud." Alex gave her a dirty look. The young woman had an attitude.

"Stoke, you're a great piece of ass. I had several great orgasms last night. I really love men who know how to please me. Thank you."

"You're welcome, but the man is supposed to say his woman is a great piece off ass. I don't like being called a piece of ass."

"Sorry. I didn't mean to insult you. Didn't you have nice evening with me?" Alex put her arms around me and waited for me to kiss her. I didn't, which surprised her.

Is this person so insecure? Does she really give a damn about how I feel? The way she acted in bed led me to believe that her own self-fulfillment was the only important thing to her. "Not really. In fact, the whole experience was a complete turnoff for me. You are definitely not a great piece of ass, Alex."

"What's wrong? I thought we had fun."

"You're a self-centered witch."

"What?"

"You heard me. You had sex last night. I was just an innocent bystander. You were the only one who got off. I was your sex instrument. It was an empty, impersonal act. We copulated like two stray dogs."

Alex slapped my face. "You're despicable. Did I somehow bruise your fragile ego? You just can't handle strong women who know what they want. I never want to speak to you again, Spencer."

"No problem." Best stormed away.

I thought to myself, what the hell was wrong with her? She actually thought we had a sensitive, loving experience last night. Actually, she just humped me and fell asleep.

The heck with her. I was going to have a good time at the party. I rejoined Rob and Donny who were chatting up two gorgeous women. Rob introduced me. "This is my good friend Stoke. Stoke, meet Sweetie and Delores."

I started to laugh and Sweetie asked, "What's so funny?"

"Your names."

"Why's that?"

"Are you gals actresses?"

"Yes."

"Do you work for Alan?"

"Yes. Most of the people here today work for Alan."

I looked at Sweetie. "Sweetie seems apropos of the business you're in. But, Delores, that has to be your real name."

Delores responded, "It is. I thought about changing it when I got into porn, but I didn't because it rhymes with a woman's body part. And that body part is so critical to my work." We all started laughing hysterically. These girls had a terrific sense of humor to go along with their big hooters.

Rob said, "Stoke, the girls asked us to join them in the hot tub. You wanna come along?"

"Nah. I'm going to check the place out." The four of them walked towards the cabanas that were set up to facilitate a change in clothes or fellatio or whatever.

I roamed about. Several women smiled at me, but I wasn't ready to make a selection. Then, I saw Amanda standing by herself near the bar. I approached her.

"So, are you having fun today?"

"Not really. Are you?"

"Not yet, but I bet I will before the night's over."

"Guys are such pigs."

"Hey, what kind of remark is that?" I looked her over. She was probably a little too young for me, and she certainly was too tall for a short guy like me. But, Amanda was a dreamboat, nevertheless. She had on a bikini underneath a sheer cover up, small, but well-defined breasts and a great body. She looked like an athlete.

"I can't believe I'm here. It looks like it's only a matter of time before everybody hooks up and starts to fornicate."

"What's wrong with that? I bet this group knows how to have fun."

"Well, I don't go to many orgies. And, why do men require sexual activity to have a good time?"

"It's the essence of our lives. Women don't get it. Men need sex regularly or they start to become mentally ill." I grinned as I said this figuring it would really set Amanda off. "And, what did you expect? Goldfarb is in the sex business. It makes perfect sense for him to encourage physical interaction."

"You're right. I should have known. However, my attendance was not optional."

"Why's that?"

"Alex wanted to attend and told me I had to join her. We want to cement our design deal with Alan."

"Aha! You're here for business purposes."

"Correct."

"And your bikini, which looks stunning, is what you usually wear while you're doing deals?"

"In this situation, it seemed to be the appropriate attire."

"Alex likes having you around, doesn't she?"

"Yeah. I feel like a trophy."

"Are you?"

"You mean are we intimate?"

"Yes, I did mean that."

"No, I'm straight. I told you that at the Design Ball."

"So you did. Is Alex straight?"

"I have no idea. You'd know her better than me. You were out with her last night, weren't you?"

"I was. Her sexual proclivities made me ill."

"Really? What happened?"

"I never kiss and tell. How would you like it if we had sex and I told Alex about it? I'm a gentleman."

"I'm sure you are, Stoke."

I asked her, "Would you like to take a walk?"

"Sure. Where to? I have an idea. Let's sneak around Alan's house. I'm going to decorate it, so we'd have an excuse if someone sees us inside."

"Great idea."

"By the way, what are you doing here?"

"I'm working on a business deal with W Pictures."

"What kind of deal?"

"It's confidential. I will tell you that it will make him a super rich man."

"He's seems pretty rich already, isn't he?"

"Look at this spread. I suppose so."

We walked towards the house and entered through the front door. It didn't seem like anybody was around. The house had a huge foyer and a curved staircase to the upper floor. A gigantic living room was to the right and a formal dining room to the left. In the rear was a great room that included a large working kitchen, a more than ample eating area and family room. The woodwork throughout the great room was exquisite.

We climbed the stairs to the second level and found the bedrooms. As we passed one of them, we heard some grunting and heavy breathing along with a woman's voice saying, "yes, yes, yes". The door was ajar, so Amanda and I peeked in and saw a two people copulating.

Amanda gasped, and the man, who was on top facing away from us, turned towards us. It was Damien!

"Dad, what the fuck are you doing here?"

"Well, I know what you're doing." The humpee shoved Damien off and scampered towards the bathroom with absolutely no humility. From what I observed, she had a right to be proud. Good job son, I thought.

Damien stood up and grabbed a towel to cover up his private parts. It was very embarrassing as he was still at full mast.

"Amanda, I didn't know you were coming today."

"I don't know what to say, Damien." She departed, went down the stairs and out the front door.

"You know Alan Goldfarb?" Damien asked me as he put on his bathing suit.

"Yes. I'm doing business with him. What's your relationship with him?"

"I work for W Pictures."

"You're kidding. Is uninhibited sex part of your job description?"

"It's one of the perks of the job." The woman Damien was screwing was now in a thong and no top. She walked past and said, "See you later D. Bye Daddy." She winked at me. "Have fun with your son. He's a good fuck."

Damien said, "Later."

"So you really did get a job with a pornography company."

"Yes I did."

"This will make your mother and me so proud. Our son the pornographer."

"Come on Dad. It's just a job in the movie business."

"Dirty movies and dirty people."

"You're being melodramatic."

"I am not. These characters are all sleaze balls."

"Then why are you doing business with Alan?"

"Good question. Maybe I should reconsider." I knew I wouldn't. "Well, I guess I'll go meet more of your fellow employees and screw one of them. Are all the women available?"

"Pretty much. Yeah, Alan told them to show all the guests a good time. Good hunting."

"Thanks, son. You should use protection."

"I'm not concerned. Our actresses are tested every month."

"Famous last words." I was dumbfounded. I couldn't believe my son was working with Alan. And, I couldn't believe I saw him getting laid. People say they don't ever want to see their parents having sex. Well, seeing your child having intercourse is worse.

I walked back to the pool area, and a lot of couples were lying around making out. The party was, in fact, morphing into an orgy. I approached the hot tub and saw Rob and Donny kissing and feeling up Sweetie and Clitoris- I mean Delores. I didn't want to disturb them, so I walked by quickly.

Then, I spotted Alex and Goldfarb speaking near one of the big cabanas. He led her inside. Oh, oh, what was up with that? Alex would probably screw Goldfarb until he agreed to give her his decorating deal. They deserved each other.

. . .

Alan asked Alex if she wanted some champagne. She agreed immediately when she saw the Cristal label.

"Thank you, Alan. What a nice surprise, a private cabana and delicious champagne."

"Glad you approve. Why don't you make yourself comfortable."

"I think I will. Do you mind if I slip into a bathing suit? It's a little warm for my sundress."

"Make yourself to home."

There was no changing area in the cabana, so Best turned away from Goldfarb and undressed. When naked, she reached into her bag and pulled out a tiny bra and a thong, donning them as she faced away from Goldfarb exhibiting a false facade of modesty.

Goldfarb loved what he saw. Best had the body of a twenty year-old and the allure of a temptress. Her ass was moon-shaped, without any evidence of ageing. He couldn't wait to see and touch everything. There was little doubt about it happening from his vantage point.

"That's better. What do you think?" Best modeled the swim-suit.

"I love it. You have a beautiful body, Alex."

"Thank you, Alan, I know I do. Yours is pretty yummy too."

"Let's drink to romance."

"I'd rather drink to a successful decorating transaction. And, I want to start the project right away. I love your new home. Is your wife pleased?"

"Who cares? I'm taking care of this place personally. I want to spend more time in the Hamptons."

"Are you retiring?"

"No, not at all. But, business has been great for a long time. The pussy business is purring. If you know what I mean. I'd like to slow down a little. I've earned it."

"Well, do we have a deal or not?"

"Tell you what. I'll make a decision before we leave the cabana."

"Sounds good. I'll try to be as cooperative as I can." Best walked near Goldfarb. He rubbed her smooth thigh as she passed.

"Why don't you sit next to me?"

Best sat down seductively. Goldfarb put his arm around her shoulders. He was thinking that this woman wasn't like all the bimbos that worked for him. She was really classy, so he needed to be smooth.

Normally, Goldfarb didn't bother with small talk when he was with a woman. He just took what he wanted because women were meant to serve him. Alex was different. She wasn't anybody's slave, but she'd do whatever she must to land a deal. And, he was going to make her work for the job.

"You have a great physique for your age." Best lightly felt his biceps and masculine hairy chest. "I love older men who take care of themselves."

Goldfarb bent over and kissed Best gently, at first. Then, he thrust his tongue deep into her mouth. She responded by sucking on it. The contact between them became more intimate and in a matter of seconds, and both lost their swimsuits.

Best took the lead, as usual, and kissed him all over. Goldfarb laid back and allowed Best to do her magic. Naturally, he became very aroused. After a few moments, Goldfarb decided to assert himself. He grabbed Best's head and drove into her mouth causing her to gag and gasp for breath.

"Take it slow, Alan. Be gentle with me, please."

"Sorry. I got carried away."

Best ended her odyssey below his waist and invited him to return the favor. His technique was unsophisticated and boorish. Best thought to herself that she had many more proficient lovers than he.

"Am I turning you on, Alex?"

"Oh yes, Alan, give me more." She nearly burst out laughing from her own words. The man was a total buffoon.

Then, Goldfarb turned up the heat and started to bite and pinch. The last straw was when he grabbed her throat and started choking her.

"What the fuck are you doing, Alan? Are you making love to me or trying to kill me? Get off of me."

"Okay, okay. I'm sorry. Did I hurt you?"

"I'm all right. You need to settle down a bit. This isn't a wrestling match, you know."

"Let's try again."

Best reluctantly agreed and counted the seconds until he bellowed like a rutting pig. Goldfarb fell of off her and breathed heavily.

"You're really something. That was terrific."

"Yeah, terrific," she said sarcastically.

Both dressed and Alex asked Goldfarb. "I hope that seals the deal."

"You bet it does. A great piece of tail always does the trick for me."

"Send me a check for 250 thousand dollars on Monday, and I'll start working right away."

"Will do. You sure were great."

"I know."

. . .

I went to the barbeque pit to get something to eat. A large pig was on the spit, and one of the chefs was cutting off chucks of meat for the guests. Swine was not my favorite meat, but I decided to give it a try. I wasn't disappointed. It was tender juicy and very tasty.

I was enjoying the sights, as most of the women were now topless. Suddenly, Amanda appeared next to me.

"Can I join you?"

"Of course. You might need protection from all of the horny men at the party."

"I think I can handle myself, but I'd appreciate your watching over me."

"Well, you are safe with me, my dear. Have something to eat. The swine is delicious."

We had a really nice chat. Before long, Amanda removed her cover up. She was really attractive, and my mind began to wander.

"Stoke, I hope you don't mind, but I'm going to take off my top and bask in the sun. Is that okay with you?"

"Absolutely, why would I object to a beautiful woman taking off her clothes?"

"Since all the other women at the party are mostly naked, I figure I can't get into too much trouble. I don't know anyone other than your son."

"Yeah, my son."

"What's going on between you two?"

"My ex-wife and I are pretty upset about his choice of careers." I was having trouble completing sentences looking at Amanda's small but perfect breasts. "He's a product of a broken home, so I guess that's why he's been making so many bad decisions."

"Were you upset seeing him with that woman?"

"I never dreamed I would see my child engaged in intercourse. How would you feel?"

"Pretty weird, I suppose."

"Maybe I should be happy that he prefers women to men."

"That's one way to look at it. So, did anything happen between you and Alex?"

"You really want me to answer that question?"

"Unless you're too embarrassed."

I was starting to really get turned on by this lovely woman. "She's a sexual predator, totally interested in her own gratification with no regard for her partners. How can I best describe her technique? She makes love like a selfish man. It really creeped me out."

"Wow, that sounds awful. To tell you the truth, she sort of frightens me. Every time we're alone, I feel like she's going to come on to me."

"You should be careful."

"I will."

I said, "I have to get out of the sun. I'm roasting."

"Why don't we use this cabana? It's unoccupied."

"Great idea." This was starting to get really interesting.

We settled down next to each other on a large couch. I was hesitant to make a move, but what the heck. I leaned over and kissed Amanda. Much to my surprise, she was receptive and melted in my arms.

You never know when you're going to get lucky in love. Who would've thought Amanda would have an interest in me? Sometimes it pays to take a risk.

I was getting very aroused by her soft lips, her probing tongue and her delicious smell. We began to grind against each other, and I touched her magnificent breasts, something that I was thinking about for the last 30 minutes. They were perfect.

I whispered to her, "You sure I'm not too old for you?"

"You're a nice person, Stoke. I can tell. And besides, with all this sexual activity going on, why shouldn't we have some fun too?"

"I can't dispute that logic."

I took off my shorts while she pulled off her bikini bottom. Amanda was at least three inches taller than me, but on her back, she was perfect!

Just as I started to mount her, the flap on the cabana opened. Guess who was standing there gawking at us? Damien. Oh, shit.

He said, "I don't believe this. What do you think you're doing?"

"Actually, I haven't done anything because you barged in on us."

"Amanda, I had no idea you were a slut like all the rest of the woman at the party. I sure read you wrong."

"Who the hell are you to judge me? Why don't you get out?"

Damien stormed away. Talk about ruining the moment. I excused myself, slipped on my shorts and chased after my son. He didn't want to speak with me.

Amanda and I assumed our seats outside of the cabana. It would have been too awkward to pick up where we left off. We spoke about the unfortunate turn of events for a while, and I promised to make it up to her, if she was still interested. Amanda said she would love to see me again.

Soon after, Alan showed up and leered at Amanda, who was still without a top. He said that Alex wanted to leave, and Amanda should meet her at the front of the house. She kissed me goodbye and gave me her number.

Alan must have been impressed that I was getting it on with the only woman at the party who wasn't a porn actress or a designer slut. "So, are you having fun?"

"Actually the party turned out to be a bummer for me."

"Why's that?"

"My son's here."

"No. Who's your son?"

"Damien."

"I'll be damned. It never occurred to me. He works for me."

"I know. It's not exactly the career I hoped he'd pursue."

"Relax Stoke. I run a clean ship."

"I'm sure you do, Alan." Actually, I wondered.

We then spoke about the proposed deal. Alan got really charged up when I told him that Donny was ready to move forward with a two hundred fifty million dollar loan, all of which would be paid to Alan personally. We agreed to speak early next week to discuss the next steps.

On the way home, I had to listen to Rob and Donny describe every detail of their sexual exploits. Apparently, two more girls joined them in the hot tub, so it was two on four. They found a vacant bedroom in the house and fornicated for a couple of hours.

Donny was ready to make the loan.

Chapter 22

Rob came running towards my office the next morning as I arrived at Pyglet.

"Was that the most unbelievable party?" We didn't discuss anything other than Rob and Donny Cohen's sexual conquests last night on the way home.

"Yep. It sure was a wild affair. I don't think I ever so saw many artificially manufactured boobs in my whole life," I laughed.

"And none of them sagged. A sea of naked breasts, who could ask for more?"

"And, when that one woman upped the ante by taking off her bikini bottom, I almost fainted." I added.

Rob was shaking his head and very animated. "Me too. Then all the other women took everything off, not to be outdone. Don't you love it when women fight for your attention by exposing themselves?"

"Rob, that doesn't happen to me very often. Truthfully, I didn't hit pay dirt yesterday. I spent some time with Alex Best's assistant, Amanda. We almost had a memorable moment, but it didn't happen."

"Why not?"

"Would you believe, Amanda and I were checking out Goldfarb's house, and we heard some activity in one of the bedrooms?"

"Don't tell me you watched other people getting it on."

"Sort of. Amanda gasped when she saw a guy humping one of Alan's babes. He turned around, and guess who it was?"

"I give up. Who?"

"Damien."

"Get the fuck outta here. Your son?"

"In the flesh, literally."

"What happened? Why was Damien at the party?"

"He was totally pissed off. The girl didn't seem to care. She was a beauty by the way. Great body. First, Amanda stormed away. I ascertained that she met Damien the other day at W Pictures. I think they planned to go out on a date. Then, as Damien stood buck naked in front of me, he told me that he works for Goldfarb."

"You didn't know?"

"SS and I knew he had gotten a job at a porn company. I just didn't know he would soon be my client."

"Wow, that's quite a story. Was it really weird seeing him make out?"

"What do you think? I was mortified. His girlfriend was great looking, so I'm proud of that. But, do I want to see him having sex? No way."

"What about Amanda?"

"I caught up with her and we chatted for a while. It was getting hot so she took off her top. Rob, I almost lost it. She must have felt comfortable because every woman at the party, at that point, was topless."

"I love when that happens. What else?"

"Well, we were very warm in the sun, so we went into an empty cabana. Amanda was telling me about her background, and I guess the moment got to us."

"Oh my God. You're more of a stud than I thought you were."

"Relax, it's not what you think."

"Why?"

"We started to kiss and hug and got completely naked. I was just about to go through heaven's door when somebody entered the cabana."

"Bad luck. Who was it?"

"Damien."

Rob started to roar. "That's sensational. You walk in on your son, and he walks in on you. Terrific. What a story."

"I tried to explain what I was doing, but he was grossed out and pissed off that I was with a woman he was clearly interested in. In fact, he called her a slut."

"What a mess."

"Damien left and Amanda and I agreed to see each other another time. She left soon after with Best. By the way, I saw Alex and Goldfarb retreat to a cabana earlier on. So, I guess Best sealed her deal to decorate Alan's house."

"I don't know what to say. You sure were unlucky. Donny and I, on the other hand, had as much fun as we could possibly handle."

"I know Rob. That's all you guys talked about last night."

Rob queried, "What about Goldfarb? Did you speak with him?"

"I did, and he's ready to move foreword. Obtaining two hundred fifty million in cash really turned him on. Get him together with Donny for some due diligence right away. I want to fund this loan in a week and then start to work on a long-term deal right after that. Donny's set, right?"

"Are you kidding? He was so stoked. I could barely control him. He was screwing his brains out with three or four different women?"

"Good. Take him to Goldfarb's place. Maybe, he can bring you on a set, and you can both learn how pornography is made."

"Great idea."

"Get the hell out of here. I've got some phone calls to make. You handle Goldfarb yourself. This deal's a slam-dunk. Right?"

"W's numbers are stellar. I really like the transaction."

Rob walked out elated. There's nothing like the combination of uninhibited sex and large fees.

. . .

The day was just beginning at Best Design. Amanda arrived early at 7:30. Over coffee, she thought about the previous day, about Stoke Spencer, about Damien Spencer and about Alex Best.

The party was wild. She hadn't ever been to such a crazy affair. Naked women, everyone having sex and she was sure people were using drugs. Even in college, Amanda never experienced anything like what went on at Goldfarb's house.

It was uncharacteristic for her to be so forward with Stoke. She estimated that he was at least 20 years her senior and not exactly out of central casting with his potbelly. But, the man had great charm and charisma, and he was obviously very successful and wealthy. That's a nice combination.

She agreed to go out with Stoke and thought it would be a fun time. Odds are that he would want to sleep with her given that she was poised to have sex with him in the cabana. What the hell, why not? It's been so long since she slept with a man, she could use some good loving.

Damien, she thought, was a good possibility before the other day. But, that situation was dead, that's for sure. After seeing him in action and then him seeing her in action, there was no further basis for more contact of any kind.

Alex was a real problem. Amanda was unsure about how she felt about her. On the one hand, Alex was touted as a spectacular designer. On the other hand, she was an overly aggressive egomaniac. Moreover, it was clear she wanted to be intimate with Amanda. If sex was a prerequisite to working at Best Design, it might be a deal killer.

At that moment, Alex walked into Amanda's tiny office.

"Good morning Amanda. How are you today?" She really didn't care.

"I'm fine. And good morning to you."

"I'm expecting a 250 thousand dollar check from Goldfarb today. We, or should I say you, are going to start working on his project immediately. I have several other deals in the hopper, and I must deal with a billing problem and a former client." Actually, she wanted to fucking kill Gordon for being such a pain in the ass.

"Aren't you going to work with me on the Goldfarb situation?"

"I'm right next door. You can do this job yourself. That's why I hired you." Best was comfortable with Amanda doing the design work. What she didn't know was whether she could handle Alan's libido.

"Well okay. How should I proceed?"

"After the check arrives, make an appointment to see Gold-farb. You should spend some time with him soliciting his ideas about the job."

"I really should go out to the Hamptons and spend an after-noon at his place. I'll be able to generate more ideas that way."

"Fine. Do what you must. It's your call. Just so you know, this could be a two million dollar purchase. And, I will handle spe-cific furniture purchases you negotiate and do all the billing. We always use Carolina Furniture. Understood?"

"Yes. Of course."

"Did you have fun at the party?"

"I did." She lied.

"You don't sound very enthusiastic. I saw you speaking with Stoke Spencer. What do you think of him?"

"He's a nice man. Very interesting, but rather outspoken."

"Well, I think he's an asshole."

"Why's that?"

"We went go out the other night."

"I know. And how was it? Did you have a nice time?"

"I thought so. We ate, did some drugs and had sex. Everything guys like to do." Best lied about Stoke using narcotics.

"So what happened to piss you off?"

"He blew me off at Goldfarb's and said some nasty things to me."

Amanda held back a smile. She was ecstatic that Stoke dumped on Alex. "Too bad."

"If you do see him socially, be careful. He's a real creep."

Amanda thought about who was the real creep. "I will. I'm surprised Stoke used drugs."

"You shouldn't be surprised about anything with that guy."

Chapter 23

"I think we have a real problem developing, Alex." Jake Sardi told his partner in crime.

"You said you were going to take care of Gordon, that he wouldn't go to the police."

"What the hell do you want from me? I had some friends beat the shit out of him. Maybe, he got pissed after we rolled him."

"Looks like it. What's going to happen next?"

"It depends. If he went to the police, they probably referred him to the U.S. Attorney's office. You may be getting a visit soon."

"Shit Jake, what am I going to do?"

"Just turn on the charm and lie. Give them a freebie, and maybe they'll forget the whole thing." He laughed out loud.

"Very funny. We may be going to jail and you're making jokes."

"Relax. You ain't going to jail. How's business? You said you had a new deal the last time we spoke."

"Just landed it. Should receive a large deposit today. Could be worth two mil."

"No shit. How much for the furniture?"

"Oh, I don't know off hand, maybe a million and a half before we tack on our surcharge."

"Great."

"We have to be careful. The client, his name's Alan Gold-farb, knows Gordon and he's been warned about our invoicing scam."

"Well, I'm sure you'll be able to divert his attention somehow." Sardi laughed again.

"I'll think of something. By the way, I have a new colleague, Amanda Lane. She's going to be orchestrating the Goldfarb project."

"Is she as good looking as you?"

"No woman is as good looking as me. She's beautiful, willowy and kind of innocent, not your type. I know you prefer women with fuller figures and asses that you can really grab on to."

"You do know me, Alex."

"Talk to you soon."

. . .

"Is Mr. Cohen there? It's Rob Viand calling."

"Hold on Mr. Viand. Mr. Cohen's been expecting your call."

"Ah, my Greek partner. I'm still sore from the weekend. Thanks for the great time."

"Your welcome. Have you reviewed the W Pictures financials?"

"Of course. The bank is ready to take the next step."

"Good. We want you to fund next week. Can your attorneys finish the papers that quickly?"

"No problem. But, I need to tell you about some items of concern."

"You're not going to welch on the deal, are you?"

"Are you nuts? It's a huge moneymaker. I'm there, with some qualifications."

"Okay. Let's hear them."

"We will fund up to two hundred fifty million of senior debt secured by all the assets of the company and a personal guarantee from Goldfarb for the same amount."

"Stop there. The security is fine, but I don't know whether Goldfarb will agree to be on the hook personally. Nobody guarantees loans anymore."

"Don't fuck with me Rob. I want everything I can get my hands on if something goes wrong. I'm not going to give this guy two hundred fifty million and let him walk away if the sky falls."

"I don't know. It may be tough. You really want me to mention it to Goldfarb."

"You trying to scare me, Rob? I don't want the deal to walk. But, I want to cover my ass."

"Look, W Pictures is worth a fortune, far more than two hundred fifty mil. You'll have more than enough collateral to support the loan. I think Goldfarb might go ape shit if I ask him for the guarantee."

"Let's not mention it now. I'll see how the documentation process plays out. If we have clear sailing, I'll drop it."

"You're a good man, Donny. I'll bring you back to Alan's place again real soon. What else?"

"The loan is for no longer than six months. I repeat, not one second beyond six months. Is that clear?"

"Crystal."

"I'm going to make it exceedingly expensive for W Pictures if they can't repay the loan as agreed. And, since Pyglet's going to be responsible for the debt takeout, Goldfarb will be after you from day one to get it placed."

"Understood."

"I also want a big upfront bridge facility fee of 3%."

"That's seven and a half million dollars."

"Did you calculate that in your head? Very good, Rob."

"Okay. I think he'll go along with it."

"Is that all?"

"One more thing. I will personally cut your throat if anything goes wrong. Nobody likes the porno business, so I'm sticking out my neck to get the big fees. If I go down, I will make it my life's work to fuck up yours."

"Why are you being so melodramatic? This isn't the end of the world."

"My reputation at the bank is on the line. Tell Stoke that he's a dead man too if anything happens."

"Okay."

"I'll call the lawyers as soon as we hang up."

"Super. Bye."

Chapter 24

I was feeling terribly depressed about seeing my son at Goldfarb's home, watching him have sex with a porno actress and him being an employee of W Pictures. I figured, why should I contend with all this negativity and not ruin SS's day?

We agreed to meet at EAT on Madison Avenue for an afternoon chat. The lunch crowd had already departed, so we had the run of the restaurant. By the way, EAT is reputed to be the most expensive glorified deli in the world. Grilled cheese sandwiches are fifteen bucks.

I saw SS walk in right before me and followed her to a table.

"Look what the cat dragged in," she said when she saw me. What a terrible thing to say to someone. After they kill rodents, cats drag them around to show off. It's sort of like being called feline road kill. But then again, the bitch hates me. I shouldn't have been surprised by her comment.

"And I was going to kiss you when I saw you. You missed your chance for a moment of intimacy with me."

"You can shove your intimacy up where it belongs."

"Nice start to our meeting," I whispered "bitch" under my breath.

"What's so important that you asked me to coffee? And, why not lunch?"

"I already spend enough money on you. Be happy that I'm going to buy you a soft drink. Sharon, why don't you be civil for once in your life? I want to talk about Damien."

I looked SS over, and she really was looking great. Every time I see her lately, I have second thoughts about leaving her. But, I knew it was a physical thing. She's totally buff. The only problem was that SS was a freaking rat woman, a despicable, nasty, horrible person. But, her short skirt and low cut blouse almost offset her negative personality characteristics, but not quite.

"He's not sick, is he?"

"No, not physically, but he may be mentally ill."

"What the hell are you talking about?"

"I'm doing business with a movie producer, a guy named Alan Goldfarb. His company is W Pictures."

"And?"

"W Pictures is into soft core porn."

"Uh oh. Don't tell me."

"Yep. Damien's working for Goldfarb."

"Is the company legitimate?"

"Of course. I wouldn't be speaking to Goldfarb if it wasn't."

"So what else? There has to be more. We already knew he got a job at this kind of company. In fact, I've been sick over it."

The waiter approached and we both ordered coffee. I asked for a wedge of cheesecake, in honor of all the cheesecake SS was showing me. She allowed her skirt to ride way up on her thighs.

"Goldfarb had an orgy at his home in the Hamptons last weekend. I attended."

"Of course, you did. Did you pick up any STDs while you were at the party?"

"Be serious. It's our son I'm discussing."

"Sorry."

"I was checking out Goldfarb's house and heard some noises in one of the bedrooms."

"Don't tell me."

"You got it. Our son was banging an actress right before my eyes."

"Did he see you?"

"Unfortunately, yes."

"Was he angry?"

"Wouldn't you be?"

"How did you feel?"

"I guess if it happened at any place other than at pornographer's home with a woman who performs in dirty movies, I wouldn't think twice about it."

I decided not to discuss any other incidents at the party including the moment Damien walked in on Amanda and me.

"Well, what should we do?"

"I don't think there's anything we can do. He's an adult. And, by the way, the woman he was with was a knockout."

"That makes me feel better. You're a pig and always will be."

"You're looking great, Sharon. You must've become a regular gym rat. You're sporting a body that's hard for me to ignore." That's the third time I used the word "rat" while referring to SS.

"You'd love to get your filthy hands on me, wouldn't you?"

"As a matter of fact, I would, but only if I wouldn't have to talk to you."

"That was some pick up line, Stoke."

"Do you want to go back to your place and spend a little quality time together?"

"What would we do?"

"I can think of a few things. We might even do some pleasurable things. We never did it while we were married."

"That was your fault, Stoke. I was there for the taking, and you turned the other way."

"Give me a break. You acted like a dead fish. Every time I touched you, you cringed. I had no choice but to move on. The alternative was to be celibate for the rest of my life."

"As I mentioned to you, I've had an epiphany regarding sex. I've had relations with several men and have orgasms regularly."

"You mean like the ones you had with me?"

"Actually, I faked all of those. Now, they're real and very enjoyable."

"Why don't you give me another opportunity? I might surprise you."

"It's against my better judgment, but why not? I'll prostitute my self for old time's sake. Let's walk over to my place."

Stoke, what the hell are you doing? Are you insane? The woman's a monster, a man-eater, and you still can't resist her? I have these conversations with myself all the time.

We considered our options, and it was unanimous. SS and I were going to have sex for the hell of it. She said it wouldn't mean anything and just be a physical experience (an interesting way to put it). Using me to have an orgasm was only a small step up from using a dildo in her mind.

When we entered the apartment, SS turned around and kissed me very hard. Oh boy, here we go. I couldn't wait to touch her.

We didn't waste any time, right to the bedroom stripping off our clothes along the way. SS donned a thong. I wondered whether she planned this whole thing. Was I so vulnerable?

I ripped off the thong and her little push up bra and started kissing and tasting as much of her skin as I could. She was literally trembling with excitement.

Then, just as I mounted her she froze.

"What's the matter? Are you okay?" I said breathlessly.

"I'm all right. Just keep going."

"Did I hurt you?"

"No. Just do it."

I did and her enthusiasm continued to wane like a balloon pricked with a pin.

"What's the matter?"

"Get off of me."

Can you believe this? "What the hell is wrong with you?" I didn't move.

"Just get the fuck off of me, right now." She buck up and kicked me in the groin.

"You're still frigid. Aren't you? You aren't having sex with other men. You're full of shit. You still hate me, and you hate all men. You're a fucking liar."

"Shut up Stoke. Get dressed and get the hell out of my house."

"You're a nutcase."

"I'm just so sickened by you, I can't do it."

"Well that makes me feel better. Or, did you just want to turn me on and leave me in a lurch?"

"That would've been a great idea. I wish I thought of it. But no, your touch makes my skin crawl, as does your technique."

I dressed without saying a word. Another satisfied customer, Stoke. I told you this was a shitty idea. You are some kind of ladies' man.

I walked back to work and thought about the horrible scene I just participated in. I'm not really a bad guy. In fact, most people think I'm pretty nice. A number of women enjoy my company and the way I perform in bed.

Then it dawned on me. You just can't go back in time and wipe out all of the negativity that exists between another person and yourself. It'll never be good with a woman that you have already split with. I vowed that I wouldn't allow myself to be seduced by SS again, no matter what she says or does. I hated her as much as she hated me, and my style in bed must have reflected those feelings.

I didn't treat her like a woman wants to be treated because I despise her. But, what the hell did she expect, hearts and flowers? Was she treating me the way a man wants to be? And, did I even care?

Chapter 25

"There's an F.B.I. agent and several other men here to see you."

"Send them in."

Four serious legal types dressed in cheap suits walked into Alex Best's office.

She knew why they were here. "How can I help you gentlemen?" She turned on the charm. The skintight white pants she wore along with a white shirt without a bra enabled Best to grab their attention.

"Are you Alexandra Best?"

"Yes. I'd like to see your credentials." He showed them to her-Special Agent Stanley Lee.

"Do you own and operate Best Design?"

"Yes. What's this all about?"

"Just answer my questions."

"If your questions make me uncomfortable, I'm going to stop answering and call my attorney. Am I under arrest?"

"No. Do you do business with Mr. Thomas Gordon?"

"I'm not answering that question."

"Did you cheat Mr. Gordon?"

"No comment."

"Did you order others to physically attack Mr. Gordon?"

"Unless you're going to arrest me, get the fuck out of my office."

"We'll be back Ms. Best. You had better contact your attorney. You're going to need him. If you decide to cooperate with us, we may be able to offer you immunity."

"What are you talking about?"

"Your colleague Jake Sardi and his friends in New York are of interest to us. If you can help us make a case against these dangerous men, we might be able to work something out."

"Get out, Special Agent Lee."

"Let's go," he said to his entourage.

After the men departed, Best phoned Jake Sardi.

"Guess who just dropped by?"

"The cops?"

"Worse, the F.B.I. They asked me about Gordon."

"What did you tell 'em?"

"Nothing, of course."

"Good girl. You better not talk."

"Are you threatening me again, Jake?"

"You know me Alex. I'm always threatening someone. It's my nature. Just keep your mouth shut. I gotta go and make some phone calls." He hung up.

Best thought it wouldn't be prudent to tell Sardi about the entire conversation with Lee. She always suspected that Jake was, and still is, connected to the mob. He was a caricature of the organization, except he lived in North Carolina for some reason.

Best could feel her temperature rising. This situation could easily spin out of control. She'd be ruined if it ever became public that she was cheating her clients. And, she might even face jail time. She decided to call Will Moore, her attorney.

"Relax Alex, tell me what happened. I'll protect you no matter what. Understand?"

"Yes."

Moore loved Best. She was the perfect client. Not only did she pay him huge fees, but every once in a while they had sex together. Moore was married, so he never wanted their relationship to go any further. And, Alex was just a self-centered, vicious woman who wanted to get roughed up in bed from time to time. He suspected she might be gay because of her aggressive technique between the sheets.

An extended criminal case against Best could be a bonanza for Moore. She was never shy about paying his outrageous per hour rate.

Best told Moore about her conversation with the federal agents. He congratulated her for telling them to get lost. Most people fall apart when approached by g-men. They were obviously on a fishing expedition.

After all was said, Moore indicated that he would come over later in the week to get all the details about her relationship with Gordon and Sardi. Moore was sure that Best was doing something illegal.

. . .

Sardi immediately called his don in New York, Giuseppe "Loco" Bocco. Don Loco heads a significant organization in the Bronx where his people sold drugs and extorted people. He was responsible for bringing Jake Sardi into the business when he was a snotnose punk.

When he was younger, the don was a complete maniac and very violent. He started trouble whenever it suited him without any hesitation. He happily accepted the moniker of "loco" from his colleagues. Over the years, the don mellowed quite a bit, but no one wanted to try the patience of the don, ever.

When Jake got into trouble, the don sent him south to start a new business. Over they years, Jake has paid Loco millions of dollars of ill-gotten cash.

"Don Loco, I have some problems."

"What the fuck did you do Jake? Something stupid, I suppose?"

"This designer broad I do business with in New York and I have been fucking her clients over for a number of years. Her business with me has been very profitable. We overcharge the rich people who hire her."

"So, what's the problem?"

"One of her clients started complaining. The fucking guy's loaded, and yet, he keeps bitching about our invoices."

"So why don't you tell him to shut his face?"

"I did, and he threatened to go to the cops."

"Oh boy. Here we go. What did you do?"

"I had some of your boys pay him a visit and rough him up a little."

"And it pissed him off. Am I right?"

"You're always right, Don Bocco."

"So, what's going on?"

"The feds got involved after the client talked to the cops."

"Look wat chu done. You gonna make my life miserable."

"I'm sorry don. Usually, a few punches and these things go away. This guy's got a pair of brass balls."

"Rats like him are bad for my business, Jake. You fucked up by not telling me about this sooner."

"I'm sorry. I didn't want to bother you with chicken shit stuff."

"Yeah, but now it's a big problem. Keep me informed."

"I will, Don Bocco.

Chapter 26

I arrived early at the office and found Rob and Donny Cohen in the conference room. Papers were spread all over the table.

"What are you guys doing?"

"Final changes on the W Pictures bridge loan," Rob replied.

"Any issues?"

"Not really," Rob again. "Seems like Goldfarb has his shit together."

"That's great. Tell me more."

"W Pictures has a locked in source of revenues from cable TV stations across the country. Because they focus on soft porn, rather than more explicit films, they get the lion's share of orders from non pay-per-view broadcasters."

"What about the hard core pay-per-view?"

"Other companies film that stuff."

"Why is that?"

"Actually, the hard core movies are much more profitable. So, there's very little competition for Goldfarb's porn lite. W Pictures has pretty much cornered the market."

"Interesting."

"Furthermore, W Pictures has a huge library having been in the business for so long. The films never lose value."

Donny finally chimed in. "The important thing to note is that W Pictures' cash flow is bullet proof. There's no smoke or mirrors or accounting games. The cable stations air the stuff, and W gets a check."

"So Donny, are you ready to roll?"

"I'm done. I can fund the loan tomorrow."

"Outstanding. What about fees?"

Rob speaking. "Donny gets three points times two hundred fifty million dollars up front. Plus, he will receive an interest rate of 6% for six months."

"Wow. That's pretty expensive."

Donny said, "We're taking the whole loan, no syndication, very neat and clean. The pornographer gets two hundred fifty large on day one to do whatever he wants."

Rob added, "But, we have to refinance before six months or Donny gets another three points and the rate increases big time."

"That certainly gives us the impetus to get a debt deal done quickly," I responded.

"That's correct. I want this loan off my books in six months," Donny replied.

"Okay, let's do it. Have you told Goldfarb?"

"He's been calling every hour. I don't think he gives a shit about anything other than getting the cash," Rob interjected. "By the way, we all need to understand that Goldfarb is critical to the deal. He's the guy that makes W Pictures click. So, we must have his personal guarantee for two hundred fifty million. This term is not negotiable."

"I see. What about the long-term debt lenders?"

"They need it too."

"Let's get it done. Good job."

Rob spoke, "Our advisory fee is 1%, or two million five hundred thousand dollars. Plus we get a fee of three percent for placing the take out loan."

"I like it."

"We'll call Goldfarb right away to seal the deal." Rob replied.

. . .

Amanda was very nervous about seeing Goldfarb without Alex. She sensed the man was a ticking time bomb, a sexual predator. She decided to be very careful about what she said to him and what she wore. Amanda donned black slacks and a very unrevealing top.

"Come on in Amanda. You look ravishing as usual." Amanda walked into Goldfarb's very large office. Goldfarb sized her up and was very interested.

"It's good to see you, Alan."

"I decided we should have lunch in my office. It'll be more private, and we'll be able to finish all of the preliminary work for my house."

"That's a great idea. And, are we good to go out to the Hamptons next week?"

"Yes. I'm working on a large transaction with Stoke Spencer and Rob Viand that should close in a day or so. So, next week is good for me."

"Shall I meet you at your home at about 11 on Monday?"

"No, no, no. I'll lease a chopper to take us out. It'll save a lot of time. We can leave mid morning, do our business and be back by two or three. How's that sound?"

"Lovely."

"Is Alex going to join us?"

"No, she's involved in another transaction. You're stuck with me. I hope that's okay."

"I'm delighted. I couldn't think of anyone I'd like to be stranded with more than you." Goldfarb thought he screwed the boss, now he'll try to screw the subordinate.

"Oh, Alex told me to thank you for sending us a deposit."

Amanda thought to herself that so far Alan was acting like a perfect gentleman. Maybe she misjudged him. She should only know what was running through his mind.

Goldfarb and Amanda spent two hours going over some preliminary ideas about the type of furniture Goldfarb wanted and some estimated costs. The latter totaled over two million dollars, before fees for Best Design. Amanda had never worked on such a large transaction before.

They ate lunch. Alan asked about her family, education and former work experience. Amanda asked how Goldfarb had gotten into the porn business. She was a little embarrassed about doing business with a pornographer, but fees were fees. She just wouldn't be able to tell her parents about this particular client.

They finally finished their business and Goldfarb showed her to the door. They shook hands, and Amanda was feeling great about the Goldfarb.

On the way to the lobby, Damien approached her.

"Hello Amanda."

"Hi Damien."

"You finalizing your decorating deal with Alan?"

"Yes. We've already started to work on the project."

"Great. I hope you make a lot of money."

"About the other day . . . "

Damien interrupted her, "Look, we're grown ups, and we do what we want to do. Right?"

"That's fine with me. I want you to know that your father and I weren't spying on you. He didn't even know you were at the party."

"I know. And I apologize for walking in on the two of you. I must say I was pretty surprised."

"With what?"

"Well, you were having sex with my father. He's so old. Why would you want to be with him?"

"I'm not going to dignify your questions about my behavior."

"Don't get huffy about it. My father is in his 50s. Do you really want to be with a man that much older than you?"

"He's mature and not rash."

"You don't know what you're talking about. He's a fucking pig. He left my mother, my brother and me high and dry."

"Are you saying he doesn't take care of you?"

"Oh, he sends my mother checks each month, but that's about it. He's never had time for his sons."

"That's why you hate him?"

"Correct. You better watch yourself."

"Thanks, I'll keep that in mind. Goodbye Damien." She left.

On the way home, Amanda was deeply troubled by the relationship between Damien and Stoke. It was so sad that broken marriages have such a long-lasting effect on fathers, mothers and children. She was sure that Damien's perspective was warped to some extent, but there had to be some truth to it. The real key is how Stoke and his ex-wife get along. A mother could really poison the relationship between a father and a son.

Chapter 27

"So, what should we do about Damien? I'm concerned," SS asked me. I hate when this woman calls me in the office to vent her insecurities.

"Well, so am I, Sharon. The porno business is populated with creepy people. You should know that Pyglet is doing business with W Pictures. I've met with Alan Goldfarb, Damien's boss, a few times, and he seemed to be an okay guy. However, I don't approve of his lifestyle."

"Stoke, the man's a pornographer. He takes advantage of innocent young women and forces them to do degrading sexual acts."

"Stop it. The women don't do anything they don't want to do. You're thinking about how the industry operated 50 years ago."

"You know about W Pictures? You've looked into the company? Are they legitimate or not?"

"Confidentially, we're going to put several hundred million dollars into the owner's hands."

"You're kidding. You actually found investors who are willing to do business with a pornographic company?"

"Yes. And, they're falling all over each other to get a piece of the action."

"What are you going to say to Damien?"

"Well, he's pissed off at me, so I'm not even sure he'd take my call. In any case, it's his life. He knows we disapprove."

"How can you stand by and watch our child be taken advantage of?"

"What exactly are you referring to? He's doing this type of work because he wants to. It's supposed to be a road to other entertainment opportunities."

"Sure. He's having sex with sluts, and he's cavorting with all sorts of low lives."

"You don't know that."

"I'm going to do something about it."

"Sharon, don't make any trouble." She hung up on me.

. . .

"How are you doing with Alan?" Best walked into Amanda's office.

"We met and had a good meeting. He was charming, in fact."

"Well don't be too enamored with him. He's probably planning to lure you into bed."

"That's a strange comment. Why do you have such negative feelings about him?"

"Amanda, the guy makes dirty movies. Young beautiful women aspiring to be actresses surround him. Alan takes advantage of these young girls."

"How do you know so much?"

"Alan came on to me." Best lied. She actively encouraged the liaison. "We had a little fling."

"When did all this take place?"

"At the party."

"What happened?"

"I'm not going to go into all the details, but I will tell you he's a terrible lover, very selfish and aggressive. I couldn't wait till he finished doing his business."

"Was he angry with you?"

"No way. He thought he was sensational and was in seventh heaven. It was a non-event for me."

"Why did you have sex with him?"

"For the deal, of course. We're in business, Amanda. I do what I must to make money."

"Do you expect me to seduce clients to get business for Best?"

"That's your decision. You'll get paid more if you bring in new clients. Sometimes a sexual favor can seal a transaction."

"What about hard work and creativity?"

"All that's important too. But, there are a lot of hard working and creative people out there. Most don't look like you and me. We have physical attributes that give us an advantage."

Best moved around Amanda's desk and sat on it. She wore a mini skirt and made no effort to be modest. She stroked Amanda's hair. It was late, so no one was in the office.

"Alex, what do you want from me?"

"I want to make love to you, right now."

"Is this part of my job description?"

"Maybe it is. I'm very attracted to you. You're so beautiful."

"I told you I that I'm not comfortable with this type of relationship."

"What do you have to lose? I won't hurt you. I'll be very gentle. You may really enjoy it."

Best knelt down next to Amanda and kissed her bare legs. The woman was relentless and hungry.

Amanda's head was spinning. She never thought that she would ever use her body to get ahead. But, here she was doing exactly that. Alex was beautiful and very experienced with men and women. She knew how to make a person of either sex feel wonderful if she was inclined to do so.

Amanda was surprised to feel her defenses falling. She was giving in to another woman. Best probed further and further up her legs. Finally, Amanda relented completely and slouched in her chair giving Best unimpeded access.

It felt so fantastic, warm and electrifying. The moaning grew louder and Amanda sang out in ecstasy. The experience was new to her. It was so sensual and soft and giving. Her body began to spasm. Amanda thought she would pass out if Best continued any longer, but she didn't have the energy or desire to make her stop. Best finally ended her assault.

Best arose and kissed Amanda sweetly and then deeply indicating that there was more to come. Both groped each other, but Amanda asked Best to stop.

"What's wrong darling? Didn't I make you feel great?"

"Oh yes, Alex. It was amazing."

"Then why not go on. You should share."

"I can't."

"Please Amanda, I need you. I'm so hot."

"No, I can't."

"You realize sex is a two way arrangement. You're being a self-ish bitch." Best's demeanor changed.

"Stop Alex. Don't ruin the moment."

"You're the only one who had a moment."

"I should go home."

"You really fucking piss me off. I give you so much, money and love. And, I get nothing in return."

"Alex, I don't do this. I'm not bisexual. I gave in to you because I was frightened not to." It was a lie. Amanda needed to think about her reaction to her boss' seduction. Maybe she wanted more. But not now.

"Don't give me that innocent shit. You knew exactly what was happening, and what I'd expect in return."

"No, no. I'm not experienced with women."

"Fuck you." Best walked out.

Amanda packed up and left before anything else happened. Her legs were wobbly as she walked out of her office.

Chapter 28

Rob Viand was in Donny Cohen's conference room finishing up the details of the W pictures bridge loan. Goldfarb agreed to every term except one, he wouldn't provide a personal guarantee to the subordinated lenders. However, he was amenable to a guarantee of the American Bank loan.

"Mr. Cohen, Alan Goldfarb is in the waiting room."

"Send him in."

Moments later, Goldfarb joined the group. He was in a positively great mood. After all, he was going to receive a wire transfer of two hundred fifty million dollars momentarily.

"Good morning gentlemen. I see there are no ladies in the room. What a pity. I should have asked some of my actresses to join us for the closing. Donny, I'll bet you would've lent me the money with no covenants." All the men looked up and giggled. "Maybe, I'll have a closing party. The dress code will be thongs only." Everyone laughed.

"Are you ready to do the deal?" Rob asked Goldfarb.

"Yes I am."

Cohen spoke up. "Alan, I want this loan repaid in six months. I hope that you understand that I will be relentless about repayment."

"I understand. But, I suggest you make it clear to Rob. He's responsible for doing the long-term debt deal."

Rob responded, "Believe me, I understand Pyglet's responsibilities."

One of the attorneys representing the bank said, "Let's get it done. Mr. Goldfarb, you have to sign in a number of places, so why don't you sit down and make yourself comfortable.

In about 20 minutes, it was over. The loan proceeds were wire transferred to Goldfarb's personal bank account. No one knew that he gave instructions for the money to be rewired immediately to an offshore account in Bermuda, which then transferred the funds into three separate accounts located in three different banks in the U.S.

Cohen called his assistant who brought in some champagne and the group toasted to a successful transaction.

. . .

The next day, Sharon Spencer googled W Pictures and determined that Alan Goldfarb was the chief executive officer of the company. She phoned the main office number.

"Mr. Goldfarb, please."

"Who's calling?"

"It's Sharon Spencer, Damien Spencer's mother."

"Just a moment, Mrs. Spencer."

"Hello, this is Alan Goldfarb. Are you really Damien's mother?"

"Yes I am, Mr. Goldfarb."

"How can I help you? You're son is doing an excellent job at W Pictures, by the way."

"You're a pornographer, Mr. Goldfarb, aren't you?"

"That's a very derogatory term, Mrs. Spencer. There's no need to denigrate my business."

"Don't lecture me, Alan." She said his name with disdain, and he noticed that she did.

"What is your problem?"

"The problem is my son is working at a sex factory. And, I don't like it."

"Well, have you spoken to him?"

"Yes. But, he doesn't listen. You've obviously filled his head with outrageous expectations. He's been brainwashed."

"I've done nothing of the sort. He approached me, and I took him on because I appreciated his ambitions. And, I repeat, he's doing just fine."

"What are his responsibilities at the company?"

"He's a producer of my movies. He expedites our production activities."

"Is he involved in dirty movies?"

"We make adult films. Only our critics call them dirty movies, unfortunately."

"Does he perform in any of them?"

"No, not yet. He's asked me for some roles."

"Oh my God. He's going to have sex on film?"

"Relax. We simulate sex at W Pictures. It's all fantasy. Men and women get turned on when they watch our movies. It makes them happy."

"I know about your movies. They're disgraceful and should be banned."

"Mrs. Spencer, this is not the early 20th Century. I'm free to make whatever movies I care to make. There is no longer any censorship."

"That's too bad."

"I have to get off the phone now. I suggest you speak with your son and discuss the morality of my business. I can tell you that he fits in well at W Pictures."

"I will do that."

"It was interesting chatting with you. Goodbye." Goldfarb hung up.

Sharon was furious. The man was totally patronizing and disingenuous. And, she was sure Goldfarb was a shady character.

Later, she emailed me to tell me she had a conversation with Goldfarb. Of course, I was furious, but I was confident that the W Pictures deal wouldn't be affected.

Chapter 29

Rob came strolling into my office. "We did it."

"Outstanding. I was really concerned."

"Why?"

"My ex-wife called Goldfarb to complain about him hiring Damien."

"Oh shit."

"All of sudden, she's being very protective of her son. She should have been a better mother years ago."

"Don't sweat it, Stoke. Goldfarb's a good man. It's not a real smut operation. It's just a bunch of nude people rolling around in bed. Really, the movies are harmless, and no women are being abused as far as I can tell."

"What would you think if your son was in that business?"

"I suppose I'd hate it."

"That's my point. It's almost as if Damien tried to select a career that would make us feel terrible."

"Kids are like that. He's an adult, so go with it. He's probably still pissed off at you and Sharon for splitting up."

"I'm happy about closing the deal. But, the work is not done. You need to get the deal placed with a new lender immediately."

"All ready working on it. I have a few big guys lined up. There's a lot of interest at the rates we're offering."

"Even though the company is into porno?"

"These guys don't give a shit. All they're concerned with is yield."

"Well, do it quickly, please. Let's not get stuck with this thing. Cohen will go ballistic and so will his bosses at the bank."

"How are you doing with my ex-wife?"

"We're going to see each other and test the waters. I'm still very uncomfortable about all this."

"It's okay. In fact, the sooner she's with another man, the better."

"Have you worked everything out with her?"

"Yes. Money on money deal. A few million, she gets the apartment and I'm free."

"That's a big price, my young friend."

"What's the true price of freedom?"

"You act like you've been in hell."

"In a way, I have been."

"You're going to regret this decision, Rob. Laura is a wonderful, beautiful woman."

"There's a million more like her. I plan to sleep with every one of them."

"I admire your determination."

Rob walked out shaking his head. He smiled as he trod past Laura's desk.

In an hour, I couldn't get Laura off my mind. She looked particularly great today in tight black pants and a loose blouse. I watched her all day as her breasts jiggled when she trundled around the office.

At about six thirty, everybody had left the office. I approached her. "Why don't you come into my office? We can chat."

"Sure."

My heartbeat increased as she entered. She shut the door and locked it.

"Sit down and make yourself comfy. Want a drink?"

"I'd love one. Do you have a beer in the fridge?"

"I do. In fact, I have two of them."

I brought a beer to Laura and sat next to her on the couch. My office is on a high floor, and we could see Queens.

She said, "Nice view."

"It is."

"Do you ever wonder whether other people have to deal with the same crap that we do?"

"Actually, I'm sure everybody has their own problems. We all spend a good chunk of our lives being hurt by others and trying to get over it."

"So what problems do you have besides trying to get me in bed?"

"Well, right now that's the primary thing on my mind."

"Seriously, what else?"

"You know I was married to a horrible woman. She makes me miserable every time I speak with her."

"Even though you've been divorced for so long?"

"Remember, we have kids."

"Of course. I forgot."

"My son Damien is in the pornography business. In fact, he works with W Pictures, the company we just did a deal with."

"Is that so. He's not an actor, is he?"

"Not yet, but he wants some roles." I related the incident at Goldfarb's to Laura. I didn't mention the part about Amanda and me, just about seeing Damien having sex with an actress.

"Boy, you must have been mortified. Watching two attractive people having sex on film could be a turn on. But, seeing a family member certainly isn't."

"So, what about us? I want you so much. I'm afraid of moving too quickly and screwing it up. I have a knack for getting into situations with bad endings."

"You don't have to worry."

"I'm not sure I can be committed in a relationship after only a few dates. It will take more time."

"I understand. I was with Rob, remember?"

"I guess you do."

I leaned over and kissed Laura gently on the lips. We hugged, and she kissed my neck and whispered something I didn't understand. I caressed her back, ran my hand through her hair and touched her in a few places I understood women liked to be touched.

She said, "Stoke, this is going to be your big moment. Are you ready to make love to me? Do you want me? Do you have a condom?"

"What?"

"A condom. Do you have a condom?"

"I thought all young women are on the pill. Are you worried about STDs?"

"No, not from you. I'm worried about getting pregnant. I stopped taking the pill a couple of months ago. I wasn't having sex with Rob, so why take them?"

"We might be in luck. I think I have a rubber in my wallet, believe it or not. If so, it's been their for a while waiting for such a moment."

"You have it in your wallet? Like when you were a teenager?"

"Where else would I carry a condom? I always have my wallet, so I always have a condom assuming I replaced it the last time I needed protection."

I rummaged through my wallet while Laura started to undress. "Eureka!" I shouted.

We kissed and hugged and felt each other up in great anticipation. My moment, albeit with a raincoat, was at hand. After she stroked me a couple of times, I knew I should sheath up.

I grabbed the condom, and was so nervous that I couldn't open the plastic package.

"Let me help you with that," Laura said sympathetically. "Here." It was ready to be rolled on.

I fumbled with the fucking gadget, and it became slightly undone making it difficult to put on. Laura sat there naked and shook her head in disbelief. I fussed and fussed and wouldn't you know it, the condom ripped.

Laura stated to laugh hysterically. What a disaster. "I suppose you don't have another one in your wallet?"

"No, I don't. Can we make love, and I'll withdraw?"

"No, Stoke. No rubber, no intercourse."

"Okay then." I started to grab my boxers.

"Wait a minute. I have another idea." Laura proceeded to give me a world-class hand job, something I hadn't experienced since I was in high school. It wasn't as good as real sex, but beggars can't be choosey.

We agreed to reconvene in the next few days at my place. I promised to buy a gross of condoms just in case we had any more issues.

I was so pleased that we broke the ice, but nothing can substitute for actual penetration. I wanted to cement this deal quickly. It was my dream to make love to this lovely woman, and I wasn't going to wait any longer.

Chapter 30

The next morning, I felt the urge to speak with Amanda Lane. I didn't understand why I had such strong feelings about her. After all, I should've been focusing on Laura, who gave me the best hand job I had since I was sixteen.

But, I figured I should keep a few irons in the fire. You never know when one situation or another will blow up. And besides, until I have real sex with Laura, I wasn't committed. Right?

Amanda is very young, probably too young for a man my age. But, I couldn't resist her willowy stature or her beautiful hair, face and legs. I got a chill thinking about being in bed with her without any interruptions from Damien or anyone else.

"It's Stoke Spencer calling for Ms. Lane." I looked up Best Design and called the general phone number.

"Please hold, Mr. Spencer."

"Hello Stoke. How are you? I was wondering whether you would call me. I'm so pleased."

After those opening remarks, I was happy I made the call. "We have some unfinished business, right?"

"You bet. But, it'll only happen if you treat me the way I'm accustomed to being treated."

"I'll treat you like a queen. I promise. Can we get together tonight?"

"Of course. I was going to work until the wee hours of the morning, but seeing you sounds like a lot more fun."

"How about we meet at Mr. Chow, on 57th Street?

"I love that restaurant."

"See you there at 8."

"Can't wait." We hung up.

Amanda thought about her impending date with Stoke. Was this really a good idea? What are the odds I could develop a lasting relationship with Stoke? What the hell?

She needed a man's touch after being molested by her overly aggressive female boss. Amanda was convinced that the woman just took what she wanted, any one or any thing. Since she was beautiful and available, Alex took her.

The problem was that Amanda found the experience to be really enjoyable. In fact, Amanda couldn't remember the last time she was so turned on. And, she never had multiple orgasms before. Being kissed in that fashion in her office with her boss on her knees was so outrageously risky. Bottom line, she might consider another liaison with a woman, but not Alex. She was far too unpredictable.

Unfortunately, her attitude might have an impact on her career. She was starting to think that intimate interaction was a prerequisite to success in the design business. And, women and men like Alex were all too prevalent.

. . .

Alex was having a cup of coffee in her office taking stock of recent events. She considered her tryst with Amanda. It was a total turn on for Alex. Amanda was gorgeous, tasted like ivory soap and experienced enough that Alex didn't have to cajole her to any great extent. She was not a prude. However, Alex wasn't sure whether Amanda was being totally honest about her feelings for other women.

Unfortunately, Amanda was the only woman in the room who found the ultimate satisfaction. Alex felt like a wreck after Amanda went home. Being unfulfilled is not a feeling she experienced very often. In fact, that evening, Alex was so wound up she had to resort to artificial methods to find release.

When Alex was having sex, she was always the center of attention and in total control. There was no rule that women were required to be subservient while making love. She always directed her sexual encounters. Until last night, that is. Amanda accepted gratification and walked away. It was sinful in her mind.

Alex was so distraught that she considered firing Amanda, but couldn't do so, not with the Goldfarb deal on the line. She thought it wiser to make a managerial decision based upon the cash flow potential of the employee, rather than her willingness to engage in sex.

Goldfarb was a terrible lover, who did very little for Alex. She dreaded the thought of having that disgusting man on top of her once again. If sex was needed to close the transaction, let Amanda get on her back or her knees or whatever.

The other nagging issue in her life related to Tom Gordon, the feds and Jake Sardi. All three posed significant risk to her. Gordon just might be angry enough to inspire Lee, the F.B.I. agent, after having been slapped around by Sardi's pals. The feds could prosecute her, and Sardi just might try to kill her.

She called Sardi, who told her he needed to come to New York. They made a date for later in the week.

Chapter 31

Despite being dogged by federal agents and her frustration with Amanda, Alex couldn't get Stoke Spencer off her mind. He spoke to her in a way that no man had ever done so before. She had to find a way to put him in his place.

"Hello."

"Hi Stoke. It's Alex Best."

"Well, well. How are you Alex? How did you get my home number?"

"I have my sources. I'd like to have a chat with you."

"About what? Remember, we don't have a damn thing in common."

"I think we got off to a bad start. You haven't allowed me to prove myself. I'm really a great person once you get to know me."

"Alex, you're beautiful, but you're not my type."

"Come on Stoke. What do you have to lose?"

"What do you have in mind?"

"How about I come over to your place right now."

"It's nine o'clock. I'm going to sleep soon."

"Stoke, give me a brake. Don't make me beg. I don't beg very well."

"Okay." He gave Alex his address, and she said she'd be there in 20 minutes.

Why did I agree to see this devil of a woman? Am I insane? What good could possibly result from meeting with Alex? I suppose I might get laid, not a bad thing, right? But, I'll be subject to a lot of crap before it happens. And, her lovemaking technique is too masculine. She'll try to make me her bitch again. What an awful thought.

I cleaned up a little. I ate Chinese for dinner and discarded the containers that were still on the coffee table. Then, I put on an old bathrobe after deciding not to put on pants for the meeting. If she wanted sex, I would be prepared. It was likely to be either wild, unsatisfying sex or a fuck you contest. Neither were particularly good alternatives. The buzzer alerted me that the wench had arrived. I told the doorman to send her up.

Of course, she was wearing tight blue jeans and a bulky sweater that would facilitate me being able to feel her up. I felt a surge of testosterone. The woman was really sexy.

"Come in. It's not good to see you."

"Don't be like that Stoke. Be nice." She kissed me on the cheek as she breezed past me and brushed her unrestrained breasts against my arm.

Alex didn't wait for me. She proceeded to walk around evaluating each piece of furniture and the design of each room. "Nice apartment. Lousy, tacky furniture, though. Why don't you hire me to redo the place? You'll be happy you did."

"I like my furniture." I tried not to be defensive. I knew I couldn't stand up to an assault from her about furniture design.

"I'm glad you got dressed up to see me," she said sarcastically. "I'll be happy to introduce you to a male stylist I know and a physical trainer," she said even more sarcastically.

"Did you come over here to insult me? What do you want?"

"I wanted to see you again. I think we could develop a nice relationship with a little work. How about a drink?"

"What would you like?"

"White wine."

"Okay." I saw her whip out her little cocaine box and take a hit. Oh boy, this is going to get crazy in a few minutes, I predicted under my breath.

When I returned, Alex was sitting on the couch, and she was topless donning only a thong.

"Alex, I don't want to be raped again. You're way too much woman for me. You need a man with a lot more self confidence than I have."

"Come over here and sit next to me." I complied.

She kissed me as soon as I sat down and thrust her tongue deep into my mouth. I felt like throwing up. But, she refocused me by fondling my private parts. I responded accordingly.

"That's a good boy. Doesn't that feel good?"

"It always feels good when a woman touches me down there."

Alex pulled my boxers off, slid down off the couch and explored me with her mouth. It was absolutely amazing. The woman was a maestro with a baton. That's poetic! The intensity increased, and I was approaching the release point. She knew it and stopped.

"I want you on top of me, just the way I know you like it. You want to be the man. You want control. Well, I'm yours, Stoke."

Now that's more like it, I thought. Maybe, Alex was a real woman after all, not a man in a woman's skin. I climbed on board determined to give her my best performance. I looked at Alex's face, and she smiled evilly at me.

"How does that feel?" I asked her. I was starting to think I was some kind of stud.

"It's okay. I didn't realize you were not particularly well endowed when we fucked the last time."

"What?"

"You heard me, Shorty. You have an very small penis for a man of your girth."

"You bitch. I knew this was a stupid idea. Why did you come to see me?" I withdrew from her.

"You needed a lesson in humility. When I make love to a man, I give the orders. You're nothing unless I respond to you. And right now, I'm not responding to what you're doing."

The buzzer went off.

"Shit." I climbed off the witch and the couch without anything on from my waist down. Alex lay there grinning like a she-devil. "Yeah. Who? She what?" I looked at Alex and said, "You better get dressed. I have another visitor coming to my apartment."

"Did you have a previous appointment?"

"Not really. It's my ex-wife. She's a pain in my ass just like you."

Alex responded, "This should be interesting." She took her time. The doorbell rang and I meandered to the door. "I'm busy Sharon. I can't talk now."

"Open the fucking door, Stoke." I relented before my neighbors became involved.

SS came barging in and immediately saw Alex, who was still topless. At least, she put on her jeans.

"Who the hell is this slut?"

Oh, oh, I thought.

"You were actually married to this pathetic imitation of a man?" Alex replied.

"Yeah, and I also dumped him after I wised up."

"Good for you, girl."

"Who are you?"

"Alex. And you are?"

"You can call me Mrs. Spencer."

"Oh, wow, you must be some high society grand dame."

"I don't like your fucking attitude."

Alex replied, "And, she's vulgar to boot."

"Watch your mouth, girly."

"You actually were in love with this mini-dicked, sorry-ass man and gave birth to his children?"

SS responded, "Stoke, what kind of women do you screw? What rock did this cockroach crawl out from?"

"Ladies, let's be mature and calm. To be clear, I can't stand either of you. I made a big mistake marrying her." I pointed at SS and looked at Alex. "And, I made an even bigger mistake having you over tonight." I pointed at Alex and looked at SS.

Both women were now furious.

"I'm leaving so you two love birds can have some private time. Try not to kill each other." Alex laughed as she put on her top and then left.

"Stoke, you're a sick man."

"Look, I goofed. Alex is an unbearable, self-centered female monster. Actually, the same description suits you. Why the hell have you broken into my home?"

"I want to talk about Damien."

I allowed SS to bloviate, scream and carry on for about 15 minutes. Then, I told her to get the hell out.

As she walked out, I said, "I'll speak with Damien." I slammed the door behind her. I actually felt sorry for the woman for a second, but then got over it.

Chapter 32

"It's Donny Cohen. May I speak with Rob Viand?"

"Hold on please."

"Donny. How's it hanging?"

"I'm feeling pretty good actually. In fact, I thought we should celebrate the closing of the W Pictures deal."

Rob said, "Good idea. What do you have in mind?"

"How about we start off with a steak and head over to a titty bar?"

"Steak and boobs, what a combination. I'm in," Viand replied.

"We can meet at 9 at the restaurant."

"Perfect. See you there." Rob had a feeling this could get a little wild. Donny was a real whoremonger. With a pocket full of c-notes, he could be really dangerous in a strip joint.

. . .

I made plans earlier in the day to see Amanda for dinner. We were going to meet at Mr. Chow at eight, my favorite restaurant in the world.

It was already 7:45, and I packed up my stuff and crammed it into my old, beat up attaché case. I saw Laura at her desk working. Everyone else had already left for the day.

"What are you doing here so late?"

"Just some busy work. It's either stay in the office or go home and watch reality programs."

I smiled. "Sounds like you're still up in the air about Rob."

"It takes time when you break up with someone. Right?"

"I suppose so. I've broken up with so many women that I don't know what the norm is. Usually, I have a huge fight with them and never want to see them again."

"That's one way to do it. My preference is to be a little more civilized, but it usually hurts more. What are you doing tonight?"

It appeared that Laura was fishing for an invitation. "Business dinner." I lied. "I take out a lot of people trying to get them to do deals with Pyglet. Every potential client wants to be fed before he decides whether to hire me as an advisor."

"Is that why so many older businessmen have big guts?"

"Now that you mention it, I think that's probably true. The alcohol doesn't help either."

"Are we going to get together soon?" She asked.

"I'd like that. Maybe we could see each other this weekend." I was hoping that Amanda would drain my resources, and I might need a few days to recharge. "Maybe we could spend a weekend together in the Big Apple."

"Sure. Let me know. I can see you're in a hurry."

"Can I kiss you goodbye?" I asked.

"That would be nice." We hugged and kissed with our mouths open. French kissing is a total turn on for me. It's very sensual to suck on a woman's tongue. I started to get aroused and decided to leave before I jumped on Laura.

"You sure you want to go to dinner?"

"Not really. But I should. My guest is waiting at the restaurant."

"Where are you eating?"

"Mr. Chow."

"I've never been there."

"It's great." I walked out.

. . .

Laura really wanted to be with Stoke tonight. She was feeling lonely. She wondered about Mr. Chow and looked it up in Zagat. "Too sexy for words ..." and "menuless ordering where 'pushy' waiters choose the meal for you." Sounds like Stoke's kind of place.

Laura decided to check out the restaurant on the way home and see whom Stoke was dining with tonight. It would be fun. Maybe she would crash his meeting.

About thirty minutes later, Laura was at 2nd Avenue and 57th Street. She walked about 100 yards to the entrance of Mr. Chow. Inside, she saw the place was very chic as suggested in Zagat. A nice gentleman greeted Laura.

"I'm Brian. Can I help you miss?"

"I'm looking for a friend, Stoke Spencer."

"Oh, Mr. Spencer is already here. He said he was dining with only one other person."

"That's true. I just wanted to say hello."

"He's in the far corner with a lady."

Laura scanned the sunken room and could see Stoke nuzzling with a tall and dark haired woman. She was beautiful.

"Would you like to stop by the table?"

"I don't think so. He seems to be engaged in conversation."

Brian smiled. "It looks that way."

"Can I leave a note?"

"Of course." Brian gave Laura a piece of paper, an envelope and a pen. She wrote a message and sealed the envelope.

"Tell him not to open the letter until after dinner. I want him to enjoy his meal."

"I will."

Laura walked out thoroughly disappointed. She knew she shouldn't be jealous. After all, she and Stoke didn't even have sex in a bed up to this point. She had no idea where their relationship would go from this point, so Stoke had the right to see other women. She headed home for another solitary evening.

. . .

"Mr. Spencer, someone left you a note."

"Thanks Brian."

"She said you shouldn't open it until after dinner."

"That's strange."

Amanda said, "You must have a secret admirer."

"I have many admirers," I responded with a smile. I stuck the letter into my jacket pocket.

"So, how do you like your job?" I queried.

"It's really great, except working with Alex can be a challenge."

"Can I speak freely?"

"Sure, I'd love to hear your thoughts. About Alex I suppose, right?"

"Yes. I think she's a self centered bitch."

"Whoa. That's pretty harsh."

"I spent some time with her and she's so aggressive, it's frightening."

"Well, she does come on pretty strong at times." Amanda turned away to hide her grin.

"It's my experience that women like Alex are dangerous to be around."

"What about men like Alex?"

"They're dangerous too, men and women who only care about their own needs. Tell me what she's like with her clients."

"What do you think?"

"I think she'd to anything for a deal. And, I mean anything."

"That's probably accurate. I don't know if she sleeps with her clients."

"I think you're fibbing Amanda."

"What do you mean?"

"You honestly don't think she's been to bed with Alan Gold-farb, the porno king?"

"Hey. Be careful. He's your client as well."

"True, but I wouldn't sleep with him. He's too old for me."
Both laughed.

The waiter approached and I ordered without a menu- gambi with squab, chicken satay and steamed vegetable dumplings for appetizers, gambler's duck and orange beef for entrees.

"You ordered a lot of food."

"I always order too much food. The worst thing that can hap-pen is to be hungry after an expensive meal."

"I guess that's right."

"So what kind of personal relationship do you have with Alex?"

"Not much. I just started working with her a short time ago."
Amanda lied.

"It's inconceivable that Alex Best is not interested in both men and women. Has she come on to you?"

"That's a very personal question."

"You're among friends. I'm just curious."

"Has she come on to you?" She asked coyly.

"Yes. It was a horrible experience, to be honest with you."

"What happened?"

"If I tell you about my travails with Alex, will you tell me yours?"
I smiled evilly.

"Maybe."

"We went out a short time ago after the Design Ball. I knew it would be a crazy date. Truthfully, I don't know why I agreed to see her."

"Couldn't resist her charms?"

"She's an exciting woman. I thought it would be an adven-ture."

"Was it?"

"You really want to hear this?"

"Absolutely, she's my boss. Information is power."

"Right. We went out to eat and she got into it with a waiter. Then, she had words with another diner. It seems she's always looking for a fight, like a man."

"That doesn't surprise me."

"Afterwards, we went to a dance club someplace downtown. She snorted some cocaine and started to act really seductive. And once again, she caused a free for all with several people on the dance floor. Apparently, the bouncers are on her payroll, and they bailed us out before the crowd lynched us."

"Wow. Sounds like quite a night."

"It wasn't over yet."

"What next?"

"Well, to make a long story short, we went back to her place because she wanted to rape me. She didn't ask me, she just took me."

"Come on Stoke. You're not the demure type. You're a player."

"That's what I thought. But, I was molested, pure and simple. Alex did her thing and ordered me around. I complied without resisting. Now, I know how women feel when they really don't want to make love."

"Anything else?"

"Yes. She mounted me and had an orgasm in just a few moments. I thought I was watching myself on a bad night. It was, wham bam, thank you sir!"

"You're so funny. How does it feel to be abused?"

"Actually, I was disturbed. I decided I would never rape another women. I now know it's not a nice thing to do." I smiled at Amanda.

"Well, at least you learned a lesson from Alex."

"It's your turn. I want details."

"Stoke, it's not appropriate to discuss this with you. I'm embarrassed."

"You really think she cares. She wants everybody to know that she has a relationship with you. She's a predator."

"That may be true."

"Okay, tell me. I want to know."

"You promise not to discuss this with anyone else?"

"I swear."

"Alex has been a little too comfortable with me. When we talk she speaks about personal things, and it makes me feel weird."

"I understand."

"Anyway, the other evening she came into my office and started making out with me."

"You didn't resist?"

"It was the strangest thing. I was really turned on."

Now, I was getting turned on. "Wow."

"I know guys get all worked up when two women have sex, right?"

"Right. What happened next?" The thought of these two women going at each other was making me insane.

"She went down on me."

"Oh my God. You're not serious. This happened out of the blue?" I said this too loud and the couple seated at the next table gave us a look. "You went along without resisting?"

"Yes. I went with it. I wasn't able to say no."

"Did you enjoy it?" Now I felt like a voyeur.

"It was wonderful. Almost blew my head off. Alex is an amazing lover."

"I don't believe what I'm hearing. Are you bisexual? It's okay, if you are."

Amanda laughed. "I didn't think so. But, Alex made me feel so great. I suppose I needed to be loved. I've been on a losing streak lately."

"I may need a cold shower. What happened then? I'm not sure I can take much more of this story. It is true, isn't it?"

"She wanted me to reciprocate."

"You didn't."

"No. I started to feel very strange and told Alex I had to leave."

"Was she pissed? She must have been lit up pretty good herself at that point."

"You're not kidding. She started to lecture me about it being a two-way thing and all that."

"So you left her high and dry, or was is high and wet?" I snickered.

"Yes."

"I need to change the subject, or I won't be able to eat." We talked about our lives, mostly my situation with SS and my sons. It was kind of sad actually, that aspect of my life was in such disarray.

After dinner, I couldn't resist Amanda. "Would you like to come back to my place for a nightcap?"

"Yes. I would love to."

"I want to be considerate and totally up front with you, Amanda. I think you're beautiful and sexy. And, I'm on fire after hearing about your involvement with Alex. I never heard a more erotic story."

"Stoke. I like you a lot. I'm not sure where this going to take us. We're separated by many years. So, let's relax and play it by ear."

As we left the restaurant, I was able to take in Amanda's physical attributes as I followed her out of Mr. Chow. Everything was a 10. Beautiful face, hair body and demeanor. She wore a micro mini skirt and a tank top. What a vision. All this and she was the sweetest person. But, I was really robbing the cradle.

When we got back to my place, Amanda immediately dropped off her three inch heels at the door, and now she was only a couple of inches taller than me.

I was hesitant to make any sudden advances. I didn't want to screw up. She broke the ice by spinning around and kissing me hard on my mouth. Her tongue was hyperactive. I loved it. I could tell she needed what I was going to give her.

I uncorked a bottle of wine for us, and we sat on the couch looking at the lights of the city from my apartment. We kissed, groped and drank.

Amanda got up and asked if she could look at the rest of my apartment. I said yes, of course. Moments later, I could hear water running in my bathroom. I snuck in, and she was gorgeous. What a beautiful, lithe body.

I disrobed and joined her in the walk in shower. We washed each other tenderly, kissed and the sexual tension continued to rise. She could see I was ready for action.

We dried off, and I pulled the spread off the bed. Amanda laid on her back with long, dark hair spread over my pillows. She looked like a layout in *Playboy* magazine.

I started kissing her head and then every inch of her face, neck, arms and breasts. Amanda welcomed my kisses in her most private places. In moments she was breathing heavy, moaning and then she sang out beautifully. I was relentless and continued on. Amanda was delirious and demanded we make love the old fashion way.

It didn't last very long and I soon collapsed in total satisfaction. I fell asleep on top of her.

During the night, we made love once more. It wasn't like when I was a teenager and was ready to go again every hour. I was in love during those special hours with Amanda.

I woke up at five, and Amanda had left. She left a note on her pillow that said she had a great time. I was sad I didn't have a chance to kiss her goodbye.

At about six, I couldn't go back to sleep and walked into the living room. I found my jacket on the couch and took out the envelope Brian gave me at Mr. Chow.

It read as follows:

Dear Stoke,

I came to Mr. Chow to surprise you. But, you were engaged with a beautiful and very young woman, probably your niece! Of course, I was a little shocked. But, I shouldn't be. We're entitled to live our own lives. See you tomorrow in the office.

Laura

Terrific, when am I going to fall in love with one woman and be happy? Never, probably.

Chapter 33

Rob arrived at the Post House a little early and sat at the bar with a drink. He was pleased that the W Pictures deal closed without a hitch. Actually, he was surprised that there weren't any snags. Deals aren't supposed to be this easy.

W Pictures was a super company from a number of points of view. The company made a lot of money and had relatively low expenses. Unlike other film companies, it spent miniscule amounts for directors, producers, actors and advertising.

Over the years, Goldfarb had built relationships with a huge number of hotels and motels, along with large cable companies. These outlets paid W Pictures an increasing annuity every year for his products.

The only issue was that the company produces porno, which is despised by a meaningfully large segment of the American public. However, you never saw penetration in his movies, but they were still graphic. There are many holy-rollers in this country that would love to ban all types of pornography. But, thanks to the U.S. Constitution, W Pictures stayed in business and prospered.

Now, Rob had to find long-term institutional lenders to repay Donny's bank. The use of proceeds wouldn't be particularly popular with potential lenders, but W Pictures' ability to service the debt was undeniable.

The only other major issue was the company's reliance on Goldfarb. He was an entrepreneur in his industry, so his continuing role in the company would be very important to any institution that considered lending to the company. It was inconceivable that W Pictures would earn the money it did without his leadership.

All of a sudden, Donny was standing next to Rob. "Hi pal. What are you drinking?"

"A little gin to start the evening."

Donny said, "I think I'll have the same."

"Well, we did it. Great deal." They clicked their glasses.

"Rob, you still have plenty of work to do. I want that loan off my books as soon as possible. If our directors find out I made a loan to a pornographer, I'm fucked."

"You made yourself perfectly clear on this issue at least one hundred times. We'll get it done. Relax."

"Okay then. By the way, what's going on with you and Laura? Is it really over?"

"Yes. We're moving on."

"You're giving up quite a lady. You sure you're doing the right thing?"

"I can't be bound to one woman any longer. I need more variety in my life. And besides, we've drifted apart over the past several months."

"Have you been fooling around?"

"No. I may be a Don Juan, but I'm not a cheater. I didn't screw another woman until after we decided to split."

"And you've broken the record for scoring since then, haven't you?"

"I'm doing pretty well."

"You don't feel bad about Laura? Do you talk to her at the office? Is she okay?"

"I think she's doing fine. She seems to be moping around during the day. But, Stoke has been seeing her."

"Are you kidding me? Your boss is banging you're ex-wife?"

"It is pretty strange."

"I'll say. There haven't been any confrontations?"

"Nope."

The two men sat down for dinner and discussed a myriad of things including sports and politics. Both finally got antsy and decided to head over to Donny's favorite strip club.

Mostly young guys, many from outside of the city, populated the club. There were separate groups from Long Island and New Jersey. Several were stag parties, and most of the boys were there to have a good time and gawk at spectacularly great looking, naked women.

Rob wondered where they found the strippers. All were in their early twenties, and they had bodies that wouldn't quit. He suspected that many of the girls had surgery to enhance their assets, which ultimately increased the tips they received. And, several of them were obviously workout freaks. You can't be buff without spending a lot of time in the gym.

Generally, there were three ongoing activities in the club. One was watching girls dance on stage. While doing so, the performers eventually stripped off everything. It usually took a while, as the dancers gyrated, teased and cajoled the crowd. Most of the men showed their appreciation by stuffing cash into the girls' g-stings until they took them off.

The bigger spenders bought drinks for girls circulating the room and might be rewarded with a lap dance. The lap dancers always wore g-strings. The lapees had to sit still and refrain from touching the girls as they grinded their bodies against the men. It's a stupid and frustrating ritual, but thousands of dollars were spent on it each and every night.

The third activity was in private rooms where anything was possible.

Rob and Donny sat at a table away from the stage, which indicated they wanted some female company. A tandem of women immediately approached them. The women were in gowns, one was blond and the other had dark hair, and they both were knockouts with big boobs.

The brunette asked, "Do you gentlemen want some company?"

Donny replied, "Sure. Sit down, please."

Rob asked, "Would you care for a drink?" The cocktails were outrageously expensive. The alcohol was watered down and the champagne was cheap, screw cap stuff.

The blond said, "Yes please. We'd like some champagne."

"Of course you would," Donny responded.

The brown haired beauty asked, "What businesses are you in?"

"We're bankers. My name is Donny and this is Rob."

"Pleased to meet you. I'm Sugar (the blond) and this is Blacky (the brunette)."

Blacky asked, "You guys must be rich. Bankers spend tons of money in this place."

Rob, "Yeah, we're rich."

Donny, "You gals must really rake it in at this place."

Sugar, "Not as much as you think."

Donny, "Do you have other jobs during the day?"

Sugar, "We're both actresses."

Donny and Rob looked at each other and smiled.

Rob, "Are you into porno?"

Blacky, "Yes, how did you know?"

Rob, "Just a wild guess. Donny and I do some business with a company called W Pictures. Do you know of them?"

The women started to laugh.

Blacky, "Alan Goldfarb is a fucking pig."

Sugar, "He sure is. He tries to screw every one of the actresses that works for him. We worked for him for a while but quit. He's disgusting.

Donny, "Is that so? Do any of the girls ever sue him for sexual harassment?"

Blacky, "All the time. But, they always give it up because he threatens to blackball them from the business."

Donny, "I see."

The conversation turned to more suggestive things and pretty soon the girls escorted Donny and Rob to a private room. Blacky was all over Rob and Sugar worked on Donny. First, the men were treated to a few rounds of intense and "hands on" lap dancing sans g-strings. Unlike lap dancing in the main room, Donny and Rob were permitted to be interactive. It got really hot and heavy after a few minutes. The girls were experts at their trade.

As the men departed, they gave the girls several hundred dollars for showing them a good time.

"That was fun," Donny said.

"Yeah. Great looking gals. They're really head masters. And by the way, you came first." Rob laughed loudly.

"I still can't believe I spent two hundred bucks for a blow job. I can go out with a dozen different women who'll do it for nothing in a taxi on the way to dinner."

Rob responded, "You only live once. And besides, your girlfriends aren't nearly as nasty and buff as Sugar and Blacky. What names."

"True enough. I think we should discuss what they said us about Goldfarb."

"You mean the sexual harassment business?"

"Yeah. I think it poses a risk," Donny added.

"I thought about that, but it doesn't seem to be a problem. Goldfarb is powerful in the industry so the girls he comes on to get frightened and back off. And, they're working for a porno company. What the hell do they expect?"

Donny stated, "We better keep an eye on the Goldfarb. Maybe you should tell Alan to cool his jets until my loan is repaid. The last thing I need is a law suit while you're marketing to long-term lenders."

"I'll take care of it."

Chapter 34

That morning, Amanda went to work late. Making love with Stoke was a wonderful experience. Being with an older man had its rewards. Stoke was a deliberate and gentle man. He had a velvet touch and seemed to be very mindful of Amanda's deepest desires. She also had the sense that Stoke was afraid to move too quickly or decisively in the throes of passion. Amanda attributed this not to inexperience, but rather, to his interest in not making Amanda uncomfortable in any way.

"Where have you been?" Alex seemed to be waiting at the door for Amanda to arrive.

"Late night."

"Really. With whom?"

"It's personal. A very nice man, let's leave it at that."

"Okay. Your job description doesn't require you to discuss your love interests with me." Alex snickered.

"Thanks."

Sensing, somehow, that Stoke may have been involved, Alex decided to dig deeper. "I had an interesting meeting with Stoke Spencer."

"When did that occur?"

Alex knew her suspicions were spot on from Amanda's question. "This week."

"What did you talk about?"

"Talk, ha, we talked for about two seconds and then we fucked. I ended his pathetic attempt to satisfy me before he was done, quite sad really. I wanted to teach him a lesson."

"What's your problem with Stoke?"

"He's a conceited asshole. He's been disrespectful to me. But, that wasn't all."

Amanda was frightened to ask what Stoke did thinking he might have punched her out. "So tell me."

"His ex-wife showed up. She came banging on the apartment door while Stoke was screwing me. We were going at it on the couch, and I was completely naked. It was a little awkward to say the least."

"Did you speak with her?"

"Sure. I told her I was sorry she had to live with such an awful imitation of a man."

"Alex, you are a cruel person. Remind me never to get on your bad side."

"Well, you already are."

"Are you referring to the other evening?"

"Yes."

"Look, I'm not bisexual." This may be untrue because she had no idea whether she was or wasn't at this point. Alex made her feel so great. "I'm not interested in being your lover. I want to work with you and design homes."

"That's too bad. We could be really great together in bed. You have what it takes as a woman."

"And you're a great woman. I came to Best because you are a legend in our industry. Let's not allow interpersonal issues get in the way of making a lot of money."

"I don't often allow anyone to tell me what to do. I had to teach Stoke a lesson. I'm tempted to do the same with you and fire your gorgeous ass. But, I'll wait and see how you do with Goldfarb. You better be ready to do whatever is necessary to make him spend a ton of dough, or you're out of here. Understand?"

"Yes. I really don't like being spoken to in this manner."

"I don't give a fuck what you like or dislike. You'll do what I tell you or you should take a hike. This is my company."

"Okay. Don't go ballistic on me."

"Amanda, you don't seem to understand. You're missing out on some really good times. It's your decision."

"It is." Alex walked away.

Amanda thought to herself that Alex was a horrible person. Her suspicions were correct. She was also very unstable. Perhaps, they could get past the intimacy of a few nights ago. If she were successful with Goldfarb, all this would soon be water under the bridge.

What was up with Stoke? Why was he messing around with Alex? She needed to ask him.

"Mr. Spencer's office. Can I help you?"

"Yes, please tell him it's Amanda Lane calling."

Liz spun around and said, "New babe on the line for you Stoke. Name's Amanda."

"A little decorum, please. Shut my door. How are you Amanda? I wanted to make you a nice breakfast. I have a great bagel store nearby."

"Sorry I left. Life's a little confusing for me right now."

"I hope I didn't make it worse by anything I said or did."

"Actually, you helped. You made me feel great, and you're a terrific lover."

Stoke wanted to scream out in joy. A satisfied customer, finally. "You're beautiful, and I loved being with you. I want to see you again soon."

"Give me a day or two to digest all that's happening. Okay? I have a question for you."

"Shoot. What is it?"

"Were you with Alex again?"

"I decided to take the high road. "Yes.""

"But, you told me you hated her."

"I do. It was a huge mistake on my part. She insisted she had to see me. I thought maybe she wanted to apologize for being the worst woman on the planet. No such luck. She wanted to humiliate me."

"Alex must have had an inkling that I was with you last night. She was trying to upset me."

"Did she?"

"A little. But, we're not in a committed relationship, so we both can do what we want. Right?"

"Of course."

"I heard your ex-wife dropped in on you by surprise. Was it awkward?"

"It's always awful when she's within a mile of me. Alex really stirred up the pot to the point that I thought the two of them were going to have a catfight or they might both attack me. It's frustrating to have to be in a room with the two people you hate most in the world."

"Sounds terrible. I have to go. Call me in a few days. Okay?"

"I will."

I thought to myself, why do my women make my life so miserable every day? Now, I despised Alex Best as much as I did SS.

Chapter 35

The day had arrived for Amanda's visit with Goldfarb at his new home in the Hamptons. When Amanda appeared at the Eastside Heliport, Goldfarb was standing around waiting anxiously.

"I'm so glad to see you, Amanda," he said when he saw the woman.

"Same here." She lied. Amanda had become increasingly nervous about this trip for two reasons. One, her career was on the line. Since she refused to be Alex's girl toy, the only reason Alex would keep her at Best was if she brought in business. This was a big test in that regard. If Amanda could convince Alan to spend a ton of money, she might be able to stay at Best Design and simultaneously ward off Alex's unwanted sexual advances.

Two, Alan was yet another sexual predator- the male version. As she thought about the Hampton's trip, there was a very high probability Goldfarb would make a move on her. If necessary, she could have sex with him and seal a deal or risk the possibility he would fire Best Design effectively ending her career at the company.

She considered the design business. Was it an industry where sex and deals were inextricably linked to each other? What about all the laws protecting women from sexual harassment?

"Come on, hop into my chariot." Goldfarb grabbed her small bag and stowed it behind the two rear seats. He sat down next to Amanda. The pilot was alone in the front row. "Okay Eric, take us to the Hamptons."

"It was so sweet of you to arrange a helicopter for our visit. It's so convenient."

"Expensive too."

"I'll bet it is."

"I'd rather not waste four hours travelling back and forth, so I don't mind the cost."

Amanda said, "I heard you closed a big deal recently."

"Did you now? Who told you?"

"Stoke Spencer is a friend of mine. We met at your party a few weeks ago. He said you were a client."

"Stoke has a big mouth. Did he give you any details?"

"Absolutely not." Amanda sensed that mentioning the W Pictures transaction was a dumb idea. She hoped she didn't get Stoke into any trouble.

"Glad to hear that. I've partially cashed out my investment in W Pictures. I worked for many years and built a great franchise. Stoke and his people arranged for me to diversify my estate," and then to ship it to another country to avoid future taxes, he thought to himself.

"Good for you."

"How are you faring with Alex? She's a tough cookie."

"She sure is. But, we get along fine. Alex is performance oriented." And, she's a sex maniac and a megalomaniac.

"I know that." Goldfarb thought about his sexual interlude with the beautiful Ms. Best. After he screwed Amanda, he'd be sure to call Best to let her know.

"So, are you ready to begin buying furniture for your new home?"

"Depends upon how this meeting goes, actually. I want to see your final plans and consider the cost. And, I want to see if there is a chemistry between us."

Uh oh. Here we go, Amanda thought. Chemistry was code for whether she would allow Alan to ravage her. "I'm sure we'll get along fine."

Alan looked forward to this meeting. Amanda was a beautiful young woman. The actresses he screwed were beautiful too, but Amanda was a lady. The others were sluts just trying to get ahead in the movie business. "We'll see."

They made small talk and enjoyed the 45-minute flight along the southern coast of Long Island. It was a sensationally clear day. When they landed, a limo and driver were waiting.

Goldfarb led her to the car. "The next part of your journey awaits you." He bowed.

"You're unbelievable. I've never been treated so luxuriously. It really wasn't necessary."

Alan thought that the money he spent would be well worth it, if he could get his hands on Amanda's body. He examined her out-fit. Actually, he was a little disappointed with her mid calf printed dress. Her breasts were covered- practically no cleavage peaked out over the top of her dress. And, Amanda donned flat shoes. Alan hoped to mount her while she wore stiletto heels. If Alex were here, she would've worn much sexier things to tantalize him. "If we can deal with each other, it'll be worth it."

In ten minutes, they were driving up the long approach to Alan's three-story house. It was a typical high-end Hampton's home, light colors, a lot of beautiful landscape including hedges that enclosed about four acres of land, access to the ocean and many other amenities. Amanda didn't get a real perspective of the property during her previous visit.

"How many square feet do you have?"

"About 10,000."

"Wow. The house is so gorgeous."

"Thanks."

They went inside and several people were already there prepar-ing lunch, which was being served in a screen-in porch. A cool breeze made the whole setting so wonderful. Amanda wished that Stoke were here instead of Alan. Everything was so romantic. Beautiful opera music softly resounded throughout the entire house.

"I thought we should have a bite to eat, and then get down to business."

"I'm starving. Great by me."

The butler seated Amanda and Alan, and the waiters brought out an amazing cold poached salmon lunch. An expensive French burgundy was poured.

"So, tell me about your background," Goldfarb queried.

"Nothing special. I was brought up in the Mid West, went to N.Y.U. and worked at a large design shop in the City. I fell in love with New York and my business. What about you?"

"Actually, my story is quite a bit more interesting than yours."

That was rude, Amanda thought. Then again, egomaniacs only want to talk about themselves.

"I wanted to become a filmmaker. So, I schlepped out to the West Coast and worked for peanuts at a couple of production companies." Goldfarb omitted his sexual harassment issues and run-ins with the law.

"Then, I decided to move back east. I hooked up with some guys, who were as disgruntled as I was, trying to make traditional movies. We decided to try our hand at pornography. The industry was beginning to flourish as Americans became less hung up about sex in the 60s and 70s.

"Finding women to perform in our films wasn't very difficult. In fact, a huge group of aspiring actresses were ready willing and able to have sex on film.

"We encountered bumps in the road after achieving some minor success. One issue was that the more established porno companies started to threaten us about stealing their business. Actually, some thugs roughed up my two partners.

"My pals were so spooked that they left town. I decided to make a deal with the powers that be that I would stick to soft-core porn, which didn't compete with their products.

"And so, my business did terrific over the years. I'm now the largest producer of soft porn in the country, which essentially means no penetration on film."

"Wow. That's quite a story. Do any companies threaten you today because of your success?"

"Nope. Now, I'm the biggest fish in the lake."

"I assume you make a lot of money."

"You bet. The scripts are, well, not complex. The actors and actresses are paid very little. Hard core actors get paid huge salaries on the other hand. My production costs are minimal. I've been in the same studios for years. I even own the buildings."

"Well, shall we get on with decorating your home?" Amanda thought she should interrupt Alan, or he might go on about W Pictures all afternoon.

"Sure. Excuse me for a second."

"Of course."

Goldfarb went into the kitchen and then returned. All of the staff exited the house, got into their vehicles and drove away.

"I asked the staff to leave for a few hours so we could have some privacy. Care for another glass of wine?"

"No thanks." Amanda could see that Alan wasn't going to waste any time. He was preparing to come on to her. She actually considered whether acquiescing was something she could live with.

If she could keep the physical stuff to some kissing and heavy petting, perhaps it wouldn't be too bad. Then, she could promise more at a later date after the deal was signed. Pretty risqué.

Amanda thought she might be able to trick Alan. But, the guy's a total pig. He expects nothing less than total all-out sex with all the fringes.

Amanda reviewed in her mind exactly what that might entail and whether Alan was attractive enough to do what was necessary. On the first count, Goldfarb would definitely attack her if he had the chance. There was no way she could justify allowing him to do so. After all, she wasn't a prostitute. Goldfarb was a very attractive older man, however. Powerfully built and presumably hugely experienced, he might actually be a great lover. Although, Alex said he wasn't.

What the hell was she thinking? She would never sell her body for a deal even if Alex did it routinely and expected her to do the same.

"Would you like a tour of the house? Follow me." They walked through the lower level, which included the living room, dining room, great room with kitchen, a large eating area and a family room, gym and two guest rooms. On the second floor were a gigantic master bedroom suite and two offices. And, the third floor had two more bedrooms. The basement contained a screening room, a billiard room and a full-scale English pub room. It led out to the yard.

After the tour, Amanda and Alan spent an hour going over some preliminary designs. Amanda had spent nearly a week creating several layouts. Goldfarb asked for the estimated cost of the project. Amanda speculated that it would be between $2-2.5 million.

"That's quite a number. What else would I get for doing the deal with you?"

"What do you mean?"

"I'd like to see you aside from business. Our relationship could be much more than just buying furniture."

"I'm sorry Alan, but I don't date clients."

"Well, suppose dating is part of the deal."

"I don't know what to say."

"Let's go outside for a stroll and talk about it."

"Really Alan, I'm not going to be part of any transaction."

"Come on, walk with me."

They proceeded in silence for a few minutes. It was very warm outside and Goldfarb suggested they go into one of the cabanas adjacent to the pool for a soft drink.

When inside, Goldfarb said, "I'm really attracted to you, Amanda. You're so beautiful, and you're such a lady, unlike that bitch you work for."

"Thank you. Please don't try anything. I'm not interested, and so it's not going to happen."

"We're just talking. I can be really charming when I try."

"I'll bet you can. I think you're a great looking man. But, our ages are so far apart. And, it's not good business to get involved with clients. It's the first thing everyone tells you in our industry."

"Sit down over here next to me." Amanda reluctantly did so, but tried to keep some space between them.

"Alan, don't do anything you may regret. The answer is no, no, no. Do you understand?"

"Sure." Suddenly, Alan made a move and had Amanda in a bear hug. He tried to kiss her, and she resisted by moving her head back and forth. She would have slapped him or scratched him, but her arms were pinned to her side.

"Alan, this going too far."

"No it isn't. Just relax." He grabbed a breast and was electrified.

"Stop, please," Amanda said in desperation.

"I'm going to take you, so might as well not fight it."

Goldfarb reached up her skirt and ripped off Amanda's panties. He rubbed them on his face like a rutting animal.

Amanda kicked wildly trying to hit him in a sensitive area. Bingo. Her knee found his groin and he doubled over in pain.

"You bitch." He recovered and slapped her across the face and then punched her several times.

"I'm going to the police, Alan."

"I don't give a shit." Goldfarb pulled his pants down forced himself between her legs. Amanda finally lost her strength and could resist no longer. It was then easy for him to penetrate her.

Seemingly, the episode lasted forever. Goldfarb raped her endlessly while groaning, cursing and slobbering.

He finally had a screaming orgasm. Amanda thanked God it was about to end. But, it didn't. Goldfarb assaulted her again and viciously crammed his face into her private area. He was unshaven and his actions were extraordinarily painful.

Then, he remounted her for another several minutes in a number of different positions as Amanda lied there. Amanda was beginning to lose consciousness when it finally ended.

"How did you like it?"

Amanda screamed, "You fuck. You raped me. You hurt me. You're a bastard." She scratched him across his face.

"Get out of my house. Now you're nothing but used meat. And, forget about decorating my home."

Amanda slowly gathered her things and walked down the driveway to the road. A woman in an SUV noticed that Amanda was in trouble.

"Can I help you, miss?"

"Yes, please. I've just been raped by the man who lives in that house."

"What's his name, honey?"

"Alan Goldfarb."

"Let me take you to see a doctor right now." The woman helped her into the car and drove her to a local clinic. A female doctor treated Amanda and completed a rape kit. Goldfarb didn't use a condom so his DNA was all over her clothes and inside her body.

The doctor took pictures of her private area and the rest of her body, which was badly bruised in a number of places. The police were notified and immediately went to Goldfarb's home.

. . .

"Just a minute. I'll be right there." Goldfarb opened his door to find two plain clothes policemen and two uniformed policemen. "What can I do for you?"

"Are you Alan Goldfarb?"

"Yes."

"We're from the police department. A complaint has been issued against you."

"What the hell are you talking about?"

"You raped a woman today, Mr. Goldfarb," one of the detectives answered him."

"That's bullshit."

"You need to come with us."

"I'm not going any place."

"You have two choices. You can come with us peacefully, or we will beat the shit out of you and drag you downtown."

"It's that fucking bitch Amanda, isn't it?"

"I don't know what you're talking about. Turn around so the officer can handcuff you."

"You'll be sorry for treating me this way. I want to speak with my attorney."

"There will be time for all that later, Mr. Goldfarb."

And so, Alan Goldfarb was arrested and charged with the rape of Amanda Lane. Of course, the sleaze ball newspaper reporters were notified and were on hand to record the incident. For sure, the arrest would be documented in the papers the next day.

Chapter 36

That night Alex Best was going to meet Jake Sardi at 8 p.m. They planned to get together in the bar at the Four Seasons Hotel, where Sardi was staying.

It was almost 7:30, and Best was still putting on the finishing touches to her ensemble for the evening. She didn't know how it would end but was sure Jake would want to take her to his room for a piece of ass. Best hadn't made up her mind if she would let it happen or not. Sardi was a rough and tumble lover, and Best didn't know if she was in the mood for that type of encounter this evening.

Donned in a skintight skirt that was four inches above her knees, Best finished off her outfit with a lightweight blouse that hung on her breasts. Four-inch heels topped it off. She admired herself in a mirror and knew that Sardi would be aroused the moment he saw her. She let her dirty blond hair drape down uncombed. It made her look ten years younger.

Sardi was already on his second martini when Best sashayed into the bar 30 minutes late. The woman was always late, he recalled.

"Hi Jake," Best said seductively.

"You're a sight for sore eyes. I should come to the Big Apple more often to see you."

"Don't get yourself in a lather. You may not get to see what kind of panties I'm wearing tonight."

"Not only am I going to see your panties, I'm going to eat them." They both laughed at Sardi's vile remark.

The couple settled into a remote corner of the bar to discuss business. Best and Sardi spoke about recent deals, how much they earned and new transactions coming down the pike. Sardi was making a lot of money from his relationship with Best.

"Alex, we gotta talk about Gordon. My people in New York are pissed this situation has gotten out of control. Now that Gordon has gone to the cops, I'm under a lotta pressure."

"What the fuck do you want me to do? He can't prove shit. The guy's loaded, and yet he decides to come after us. We should just ignore him, and the whole thing will blow over."

"That ain't good enough. We have to do more."

"What are you suggesting?"

"I'm going to put a bullet in his head and end all this fucking nonsense."

The men at a nearby table heard Sardi and looked at the couple.

"Jake, don't be so loud. You can't just talk about killing some-one in a public place."

Sardi laughed. "Those are my guys, Alex. Don't worry, they won't squeal on us. In fact, one of them just might be the one who pulls the trigger and kills Gordon."

"Why do you have bodyguards? Are you afraid I might try to knock you off?"

"Not you, but other people. Let's go up to my room so we can be alone. How 'bout it?"

"Sure. Why not?"

"Sardi winked at the men, and they smiled at their buddy. The couple made their way to the elevator and got off at Sardi's floor.

When the door closed to his room, Sardi grabbed Alex's ass from behind. "So firm, I love it."

"Keep your fucking hands off of me. We need to discuss the Gordon thing."

"Don't start ordering me around, Alex. I told you before. I do what I want. Nobody tells me shit."

"Do you really think you can just fuck me whenever you feel like it?"

"Yes, I do."

"Well, forget about it."

"About Gordon. You fucked up that whole situation. If you would have been more careful about the billing, he wouldn't have gone to the police."

"What the hell are you talking about? You had your thugs beat him up. What did you think he was going to do? He's a powerful man."

"Don't talk down to me, Alex." He gave her a little shove to emphasize his point.

"You bastard. Don't you dare put your hands on me." She slapped him across the face.

"Think you're a tough bitch, huh?" He shoved her a few more times and let her punch at his face. He was unmoved."

"I grew up on the streets of this city. I never let a broad talk down to me."

Best knew that she was getting in over her head. Sardi was a punk and a wise guy. He wouldn't hesitate to beat her up if she continued to give him lip.

"Jake, I'm sorry. I don't like anyone to hassle me. Let's start over," she said sensuously.

"That's more like it." Sardi grabbed her around the waist and kissed her hard. He thrust his thick tongue down her throat.

Predictably, Sardi soon had his hands up her skirt and herded her to the couch where they plopped down. Best was becoming increasingly annoyed about the way he was manhandling her. Her previous experiences with Sardi were much less violent.

"Jake, slow down, will you please? Be gentle with me. I'm not one of the typical whores you screw."

Sardi responded by groping her breasts and then tried to pull off her g-string.

"Why don't you allow me to take my clothes off? No need to rip them from my body."

"Good idea. Get undressed."

"Okay, okay."

Best stripped down to her g-string while Sardi looked at her hungrily.

"Get over here."

"If you keep acting like a fucking beast. You're not going to get laid. Treat me right, or I'm going to leave."

"Fuck you. You ain't going no place. Come here, I said."

Best complied. She thought she might just have to grin and bear the whole thing.

Sardi flung her down on the couch and grabbed her crotch while simultaneously snapping off the g-string.

"Go easy, Jake."

Sardi pulled his pants down and attempted to penetrate Best. Her reaction was to resist. For this, Best earned a slap in the face. Now, Best knew she was in grave danger. So she acquiesced.

Sardi was disgusting and hurtful. As he finished, he soiled her with his ejaculate.

"That was really gross, Jake."

"You deserve it."

Finally, he allowed Best to get up. She limped towards the bathroom to wash off his excrement. She was totally grossed out. In the bathroom, Best saw the swelling on her face. She looked terrible. The rage within her began to rise. No way any man was going to treat her this way.

After cleaning up, Best walked back into the living room to retrieve her clothes.

"How was it bitch?"

"You're a regular Don Juan. Do you always beat up your dates?"

"Only when they're pathetic sluts like you. You love the rough stuff, don't cha?"

Best noticed a letter opener on the desk. Thinking she might need to protect herself, she brought her things to the desk and started to dress.

"Want to go another round, Alex?"

"No thanks. I prefer to be ravaged only once a day by pigs like you."

"Maybe I want to fuck you again." He began to approach Best. She grabbed the letter opener and stabbed Jake in the middle of his chest. It was a direct hit, and the blade punctured his aorta. When he fell back gasping for breath, Best knelt down and stabbed him in his big gut and then in his left eye.

Best quickly dressed and left the room. As she passed through the lobby, Jake's boys saw her rushing out. They immediately sensed that something was wrong and went to Sardi's room. They knocked. No answer.

The thugs then went to the front desk and had someone open Jake's room. There he was, all bled out on the floor. He was nude.

. . .

After contacting Don Bucco's right hand man, the thugs proceeded to Alex Best's apartment. Upon arriving, the men bullied the doorman, who, after a few threats told them Best's apartment number. The men suggested that the doorman leave immediately and not speak with anyone about them. They told him they would kill him and his entire family if he said anything to the cops. He ran out the door.

When they reached the apartment, one of the men knocked on the door.

"Yes?"

"We have a package for you, Ms. Best."

"Just a moment."

Best opened the door, and the men barged in. One of them grabbed Best and put his hand over her mouth.

"Do you know who we are?"

Best shook her head in the affirmative.

"Did you kill Sardi?"

Best shook her head in the negative.

"You're a fucking lying bitch."

Best began to struggle, but the man holding her weighed at least three hundred pounds, and she was helpless.

"I think we should fuck this broad to death. She's really good looking."

"Yeah, good idea."

"What do you think Blondie? Can you take us both on?"

The man who held her took his hand off her mouth.

Best responded, "Look guys, I have a lot of money. I'll give you ten times whatever you're being paid."

"If you fuck us, I might consider it."

"Okay. I'll do whatever you want. Just don't hurt me. Okay?"

The men proceeded to strip Best and themselves. They dragged the woman into the bedroom and for an hour raped her mercilessly. Best was barely able to remain conscious during the ordeal.

After it ended, one man asked her where she kept her money and jewelry. "Will you leave if I tell you?"

"Of course. That was the deal." Best told them where her safe was located and the combination.

The men collected the loot as Best looked on. When they were finished, they approached her.

"Sorry Blondie. We gotta kill you. Thanks for the money and jewelry."

Best's eyes widened as one of the men drew a handgun out of his pocket. He put a pillow over her face and shot her through the pillow. The men exited.

Chapter 37

The next day, the New York Post was chock full of stories that were of great concern to me.

The first was about the murder of Alex Best. The news article read as follows:

The founder and CEO of Best Design, a nationally renowned home design company was found murdered in her apartment last night.

The police, who were alerted to an assault by the building's doorman, discovered the body of Alexandra Best, 37, just after midnight.

Police sources indicated that Ms. Best was shot in the head, execution-style, and that she was brutally raped before her death.

Ms. Best recently hosted the Design Ball, a gala event with over one thousand attendees, which raised money for aspiring designers. She was prominent in social circles and dated many famous men in Manhattan.

The police are investigating the crime and have not named any suspects.

I considered the demise of Alex Best. She was a talented and beautiful woman, but not a person I cared to be around. My one-night stand with her was creepy and unsatisfying. Alex was a sexual animal and an egomaniac. I won't miss her.

On the other hand, her death was violent, and I doubt that she deserved such a fate. But, you never know. Perhaps she infuriated a man who then shot her. Sounds pretty drastic for a domestic quarrel. Or maybe, she was mixed up in some nefarious activity related to her business. A gun shot execution is the moniker of dangerous people. In any case, farewell Alex.

The next story foretold a lot of trouble for Pyglet, Rob and me. It read as follows:

Alan Goldfarb, CEO of W Pictures, a pornographic film producer, was arrested yesterday and accused of raping a woman. The name of the victim has been withheld as it is in all rape cases.

Goldfarb allegedly molested a young woman in her 20s at his newly purchased house in the Hamptons.

He was freed on $5 million bail later in the day.

Goldfarb has made a fortune producing soft-core movies for late night television. Sources estimate his company has revenues in excess of several hundred million dollars.

Now this situation was a real problem. Certainly, it didn't surprise me that Goldfarb raped a woman. He probably assaulted all of the actresses that worked for him. In fact, I'd bet he asked one of them to come out to the Hamptons to "christen" his new home, and she objected when he attacked her.

Goldfarb should only know that Damien already rang the bell in his new digs.

I suspected that Goldfarb would eventually offer the victim a few thousand dollars and a lead role in his next heater flick. I hoped it wouldn't be a big deal.

I doubted all this would have a material impact on Pyglet's efforts to issue new debt for W Pictures to repay Cohen's bridge loan. However, a jail sentence would be completely different story. Goldfarb's extended absence from the business could bring down the company as he was a one-man show.

At that moment, Rob came streaking into my office. "Have you heard about Goldfarb?"

"Just read the story in the newspapers. Is this a problem? He probably forced himself on one of his actresses."

"Wrong, Stoke."

"What really happened? I hate to ask."

"You don't know who his victim was, do you?"

"Stop bullshitting me. Who's the victim?"

"Amanda Lane, Alex Best's assistant."

"Oh my God. What was she doing with that sleaze bucket?"

"Best Design was renovating his house. She was on the account."

"Did you hear about Alex Best?"

"Yeah. Just terrible," I responded. "I wonder if Best's murder is somehow related to Amanda and Goldfarb."

"Seems like a horrible coincidence to me."

"How did you find out about Amanda?"

"Cohen went ape shit this morning when he got the news. He contacted some friends who know the cops in the Hamptons."

"The rape charge is going to be a real issue if Goldfarb is eventually convicted of a crime. He's going to do some serious time." I speculated.

"I suppose if it was one of his employees, it won't be so bad." Rob predicted.

"Yeah, he'd probably just bribe her to not testify against him."

"Rob responded, "If Amanda goes for the jugular, jail time is a real possibility."

I asked, "What happens to W Pictures without the head pornographer?"

"It's fucked. He does it all. Our deal's a bust. Cohen may commit suicide."

"Can the company be sold or liquidated?"

"I guess so, but only at a bargain basement price."

"I put my head into my hands. "Oh shit, we're going to get our asses handed to us by Cohen's bank and our competitors."

"I'm afraid so."

"How do you feel about your due diligence?"

"What are you saying?"

"I think you rushed into this deal, and now we're in deep shit."

"That's crap, Stoke."

"The man's a pornographer. He's a sex maniac, who bangs all the women that work for him. It was inevitable that one of them would bring charges at some point. Did you run him down legally?"

"Peripherally."

"Not good enough. You've always been so careful. Now this. Is it because you generated the deal personally?"

"I don't like what you're insinuating."

I responded, "I don't like your performance. Get out and find a solution that will bail out Pyglet." Rob turned and walked out dejected.

I couldn't believe that Amanda was involved with Goldfarb. What was she thinking? I called Amanda's cell phone and got her voice mail. I told her that I heard about what happened and said I would do anything to help her.

I thought about our relationship. Would I be able to be intimate with her again after what happened? I wasn't sure. First of all, that scumbag ravaged her. Second, she's going to have all sorts of psychological problems about this sordid affair. I needed to tread carefully. Certainly, I will try to be helpful. But, there were so many conflicts to consider.

Well, that's a nice situation that just went down the crapper.

My phone rang. Liz screamed out that Donny Cohen was on the phone.

"Donny, sorry to hear about Goldfarb."

"Do you fucking guys know what your doing?"

"Whoa, slow down partner."

"Did you and Rob even consider that Goldfarb was a rapist?"

"If you're going to continue to scream at me, I'm hanging up."

"Don't hang up on me. I'm in deep trouble at the bank. I need to work this thing out, or I'm out the door. Management is going wild about a bridge loan to a company that makes dirty movies."

"I told Rob to figure something out. Maybe we can sell the operation and get your loan repaid."

"What did Rob say about losing Goldfarb?"

"The company's toast. He's the guy. But, they still have great cash flow and no other debt but your loan."

"I'll call Rob."

I looked up and Laura was standing in front of my office. I waved her in.

"Hi. It sees like something is wrong. Are you and Rob okay?"

"We have a problem with the deal we just closed with W Pictures."

"The pornography company?"

"Yeah, that one."

"What happened?"

"The owner raped a woman."

"That's terrible. Was he arrested?"

"Yes. And, it appears he will be going to jail."

"So, your deal's in trouble?"

"It sure is? How are you doing?"

"Thank you for asking. Rob and I spoke. It was horrible. He's on a high and wants me out of his life."

"You expected that, didn't you?"

"I suppose, but it's tough to hear it. I've been thinking that maybe I should look for another job. The office is very tense. You don't need me around right now."

"No, no, no. Don't leave. I want to see you."

"What about the woman I saw you with the other night?"

"Actually, she was the woman Alan Goldfarb raped."

"Oh boy. Sorry."

"We should get together. How about tonight."

"I don't know."

"Are you going to move on with you life or not?"

"Okay. Let's leave together after work."

"Deal."

Chapter 38

Donny Cohen was summoned to his boss's office. Dan Jamison, Executive Vice President, was in charge of all lending activities at American Bank.

"Can I come in?"

"Sure. Sit down."

"I suppose this is about W Pictures."

"Correct. We got a real issue, Donny. You assured me this piece of shit loan would be off our books in a matter of weeks. Now, the fucking CEO has been arrested for raping a bimbo."

"Actually, the woman is not one of his bimbos."

"Even worse. If he were hitting on one of his sluts, he would be able to buy his way out of this mess. Do you know the victim?"

"She works for Alex Best. The woman who was murdered last night."

"Oh great, a two-for. You really fucked this up. You're in jeopardy, Donny. Get back to me tomorrow with a plan for the company."

"Okay."

When Donny got back to his office he called Rob Viand.

"Mr. Viand's office."

"Tell him it's Donny Cohen."

"Yeah."

"What's the plan Rob? I'm under the gun here at the bank. Just met with my boss. He wants action."

"We can't do anything until we find out what happens to Goldfarb. You're stuck with the loan in the meantime."

"I depended on you. You hosed me for the fees."

"Please. My rep's on the line too. I just had an unpleasant conversation with Stoke. He just might kick my ass out. In fact, I may tell him to go screw himself and leave."

"You can't do that. You gotta bring this thing to a conclusion. You owe me."

"You're a big boy, Donny. Just go with the flow. I don't owe you a damn thing. Nothing is going to happen for a while, so cool your jets."

. . .

Amanda Lane was back in her apartment. She just got the news that Alex was murdered. What a day, raped and then her boss was executed, she thought.

Lane had already made up her mind that she wasn't going to let this terrible episode ruin her life. However, she was determined to put Goldfarb in jail for a long time. In this regard, she had already hired an attorney.

She was going to go home to her parents and recover for a few months and then decide what to do with her life. Presumably, she would come back to New York and find a position with another design company.

She felt horrible about Alex. What could she have been involved in to cause this to happen? It would probably come out at some point.

Stoke Spencer called. She debated whether to call him back. How did he know she was Goldfarb's victim, anyway? She decided to find out.

"Mr. Spencer's office."

"It's Amanda Lane for Mr. Spencer."

"Hold on, please."

"Hi. Are you okay?"

"I'm as good as can be expected. How did you know it was me?"

"I told you we did a deal for Goldfarb's company. It's now in trouble. We needed to find out what kind of woman was pressing charges. And, it's you."

"Sorry about that."

"Did he hurt you?"

"Yes."

"In what ways?"

"He brutalized me, Stoke." Amanda started to cry.

"I feel so bad. Why did you get yourself into such a precarious situation with this man?"

"I'm in business. The guy's a client. Do I need to worry about every person I do business with raping me?"

"Maybe so. Is there anything I can do to help you?"

"You don't want used merchandise."

"Don't speak like that. It's not that way."

"Oh yes it is, Stoke."

"I don't know what else to say. Can I see you?"

"No, I'm going to make sure that pornographic bastard goes to jail."

"I'm here if you need me."

"Thanks, Stoke. I enjoyed being with you. Goodbye."

I recounted my conversation with Amanda. The woman was a mess. There wasn't anything I could do for her. It was almost a relief that I wouldn't have to get immersed into all of Amanda's problems.

"Stoke, your son's on the line."

"Damien. Are you all right?"

"Not really. Goldfarb raped a woman and got arrested."

"I know. He's a bad guy, son. You shouldn't be involved with people like him. We did a deal with Goldfarb, and the whole thing is blowing up."

"Well, I'm out of a job. Everyone at W Pictures' main office was fired."

"Sorry about that. You should find a legitimate company to work for."

"I figured you'd say that. Nothing I do is ever good enough for you, is it dad?"

"Don't say that. It's untrue. I love you, but you don't give me a chance to help you."

"Yeah, maybe I can introduce you to another one of my female friends, and you can screw her."

I said, "Goldfarb raped Amanda."

"Oh, I'm sorry. Too bad. That's what you get if you're not careful."

"What are you going to do now?"

"I don't know. I'll let you know so you can advise me. Bye." He hung up.

It's so horrible to have a lousy relationship with your children. Every parent is responsible for protecting and guiding their progeny. When you get off track, it's impossible to do your job. And, if the situation deteriorates when your child is an adult, it's nearly impossible to ever fix it.

My life has been full of many rewarding moments, but so few have involved my family. From the get go, SS has tormented me and worked diligently to get my sons to turn against me. I haven't come through for my children as they grew up because I spent so much time building my career. Now what do I have- an ex-wife who hates me, as much as I hate her, two boys I never see and a business on the brink of disaster?

Regarding the latter, I need to reemerge myself in Pyglet operations because I'm the only person I can trust. Rob was so intent on closing the W Pictures deal that he didn't do enough analysis relating to Alan Goldfarb's character. Now, we have a disaster on our hands. Could it be that Laura has come between Rob and me? I need to consider this contingency.

Chapter 39

I spent the entire day thinking about W Pictures and discussing alternatives with Rob Viand. I detected in Rob serious reservations about a number of options relating to restructuring the company. Generally, he was reluctant to move forward with any plan that implied he didn't do his job properly.

We had a down and dirty conversation late in the day.

"So, where are we, Rob?"

"I've been in touch with the attorneys representing W, Goldfarb and the bank. The venom between them is going to make the situation impossible to clean up without contentious negotiations."

"Let's break it down. What does W want?"

"It's interesting because the W attorneys are representing the company at the expense of Goldfarb even though he's the sole stockholder. Goldfarb's representatives are only interested in protecting his money. By the way, the location of said cash is unknown at this time. And, of course, the bank wants its loan repaid immediately."

"I can understand each party's objective. Goldfarb's people fascinate me. Are they suggesting that Goldfarb didn't commit any crimes as W's CEO, so he shouldn't be required to return the money he received from the recapitalization of the company?"

"Correct. I'm unable to contradict the logic myself although he guaranteed the loan personally. If he committed fraud okay, send the money back. But, Goldfarb raped Amanda. That doesn't have anything to do with W Pictures."

"So, where do we go next?"

"I think we should sell the business."

"How can that be a sound strategy without Goldfarb's leadership?"

"Let me explain. The company has a portfolio of soft smut that generates dependable cash flow. Maybe we're over thinking the importance of Goldfarb relating to the existing business. The movies will sell over and over again with minimal marketing."

"So, how does all this affect the value of the company?"

"The value is diminished by Goldfarb's absence because he won't be around to make new movies or sell to new outlets. But, his existing library is valuable from a cash flow perspective."

"I get it. We sell the company based upon expected discounted cash flow from its current inventory of movies."

"That's my plan."

"But, won't all the existing customers demand discounts knowing they have W over a barrel."

"For sure, but we only have to sell the cash flow for and amount equal to or greater than the outstanding loan to the bank."

"You think the proceeds will be greater than two hundred fifty million dollars?

"I hope so."

"Okay. You should move forward on that basis. Maybe you can get a concession from Goldfarb for a hundred million or so to cover a shortfall."

"That's a good idea, Stoke."

"I want to talk about us for a moment."

"Do we have to?"

"Yes. We've been partners for a long time, and I can't work this way."

"What the hell do you want from me?"

"Loyalty, friendship, creativity and unpretentious behavior."

"That's a lot to ask for at this time after all that's taken place."

"I know. But, if you can't do it I want you to pack up your shit and take a hike."

"Wow. Those are pretty strong words. I guess all these years don't mean very much to you."

"Wrong. They mean everything. I'm only asking for what we used to have. You blew this deal."

"What the hell are you talking about?"

"You broke up with Laura, and you changed."

"Oh, so that's what this is all about. It always reverts back to sex with you, doesn't it Stoke?"

"I'm not talking about me. You're different. You're too cocky, too self-assured, overly aggressive and above the details."

"And what about you? I've been bored shitless hearing about all your amorous escapades over the years. When do you ever focus on details? Never."

"I own the company, Rob. I gave you an interest in Pyglet because I love you like a son. You fucked up."

"Bullshit. You gave me ownership because I earned it."

"Right, and I can take it away just as quickly if I care to."

"Maybe I need an attorney."

"No, not really. Just read the stockholders' agreement you signed."

"Stoke, have you turned on me because of Laura?"

"No."

"I think it is the reason. If so, there's no chance of us reconciling."

"That's not true. You need to fess up to your missteps. You need to morph back into my principal dealmaker. Think about it."

"I will." Rob walked out.

Was this really the end of my relationship with Rob Viand? I was saddened to think that maybe it was over. Rob's a great deal person, and he was a great friend. But, he must remember we're all nothing but expendable office boys in this business. I can train a new hot shot in six months to take his place.

And what about Laura? I guess I will find out soon enough. We're scheduled to go out in less than an hour.

Chapter 40

At seven, Laura came by my office. "Are you ready to leave?"

"Yes. I'm just cleaning up. In about five minutes I'll pick you up." I noticed that Laura was wearing white pants, my favorite. When she turned around to walk away, I saw the line of her thong through the pants. Was it a coincidence?

It was one of my worst days at Pyglet exceeded only by the time that Gil Richards, a former client, was murdered after being arrested. The impact of the W Pictures situation would be serious and long lasting. Due diligence was an extremely important aspect of a banker's role in a deal. It wasn't fun or exciting. If not done properly, a seemingly good deal might bring down the house.

Rob didn't give enough consideration to two things relating to Alan Goldfarb. One, he was a one-man show. If something happened to the founder, leader and inspiration of W Pictures, the value of the company would drop precipitously along with its ability to meet its obligations. Two, the character of Goldfarb was not at a level to deserve the type of deal that Rob structured. It was bad enough that W was in the porno business. Most banks wouldn't deal with the company for that reason alone. But, Goldfarb was a serious sexual predator. I wouldn't be surprised if a long line of current and former female employees came forward and claimed they were also abused.

So, the questions I needed to answer were in what direction should I take W Pictures and what should I do with Rob?

Regarding the former, I think Rob has the right strategy. He usually comes through in the clutch. His analytical mind was a real asset. We should try to sell W based upon its existing cash flow and current client base. It was foreseeable that a discounted sale price would cover the existing bank loan, which was all I really cared about. Of course, I could manage the process alone.

The latter question is more complex. I felt the need to jettison Rob from Pyglet. However, I didn't know if my thoughts were pure and analytical. I know that my relationship with Laura was having an impact. Surely, I would be able to court Laura more effectively without Rob around.

Pyglet has a great reputation that will be soiled as the word of this deal hits the street. Somebody's head needs to roll to restore confidence in my company. Rob blew it, so he should suffer the consequences.

As I look back, Rob's forte wasn't new business. I was the driving force behind almost all of the significant deals at Pyglet. Rob executed them. Granted, he was a superb closer. I decided at that moment, Rob was out.

After putting the last item in my briefcase, I thought I wouldn't take it with me tonight and set it beside my desk.

"Are you ready?" I hollered across the empty office.

"Coming." I hoped she would say the same thing to me later in bed, I thought evilly.

We trundled along chitchatting about the W Pictures debacle. Laura was very interested in what had transpired. And, she seemed concerned about Rob's role in the transaction. I indicated that he was the main person on the account, not I.

"So, is everything cool between you and Rob?"

"No," I responded. "He didn't do his job."

"What do you mean?"

"He was anxious to close the deal, like an amateur or a newbie in our business. His immaturity shone through and he besmirched the reputation of Pyglet along the way."

"You're not going to fire him, are you?"

"That's exactly what I'm going to do."

"Come on Stoke. He made one mistake. How can you be so harsh?"

"It's more than the deal. I find his whole demeanor unsettling. I'm totally pissed about how he dealt with you, to be frank."

"My relationship with Rob is none of your business. It should have no impact on his job performance assessment."

"It does to me. His insensitivity towards someone he loved was appalling. I have to assume he would treat me the same way in the future."

"How's that?"

"With disrespect and arrogance. This will be a good lesson for Rob. He's not the greatest banker that ever lived, although he thinks he is."

"Why are you being so cruel?"

"Laura, who do you think brings in almost all of the significant business in Pyglet?"

"I suppose you do."

"Correct. And what is the most important aspect of investment banking?"

"Making fees."

"True, but new business development precedes everything else. No new business, no fees."

"So, what does Rob do at Pyglet?"

"He executes my deals. Very well, I might add."

"Then, what's your problem? You're a great team."

"Rob finally had an opportunity to be the deal originator. He was blinded by the situation and embarrassed me in the process."

"Stoke, are you firing Rob because of me? If you are, I'm going to quit right now."

"No." I lied. "I want you to stay. You're loyal, and you're lovely. Honestly, my feelings for you did have some impact on my decision."

At that moment, Laura turned, hugged me and kissed my passionately. I could taste her tears as our lips met.

"I want you so badly, my darling. You're the only substantive woman in my life. You have soul. All the others were devoid of true affection and respect. You have always been a great employee and friend."

"I don't know about all that, but I truly appreciate your vote of confidence and your sentiments."

"Let's get something to eat."

We had a wonderful dinner at a sweet, and very old place on Third Avenue called Isle of Capri. It wasn't fancy, just good food and a little privacy. We discussed every aspect of Laura's background, education and experiences at Pyglet. We even had a few laughs about all the thong references.

The moment of truth had arrived. I asked Laura, "Would you like to come back to my place."

"Yes, very much."

We walked to my apartment. I said hello to the doorman who smiled at me approvingly.

In my home, we both tried to relax. The implications for what would happen this evening were going to have a profound effect on our lives. I fetched two glasses of wine and brought them into the living room. The lights of the city were beautiful as they always were. Laura was sitting on the couch deep in thought.

"So, what are you thinking about?" I asked her, as I handed her a glass of wine.

"I'm so afraid of what lies ahead."

"Don't be. We're all going to be just fine."

"Stoke, my life is in such disarray. My marriage fell apart, and I'm really sad about it. I also feel terrible for Pyglet and Rob."

"Let me worry about Pyglet. Trust me, I'm going to make more money than ever without Rob. I've been on sabbatical for the last couple of years. I'm going to jump back into the fray. As far as you're concerned, you just need someone to love, and someone who'll return the favor."

"You're right. I'd like to take a shower. It's been a long day. Is that okay? Am I being to presumptuous?"

"Are you kidding? I was feeling a little sticky myself. Mind if I join you?"

"That would be great." She smiled tenderly at me.

We stripped down in my bedroom and hugged each other. I kissed Laura deeply and felt her melt in my arms. She really needed my affection.

We entered my shower and lathered up. It was glorious. She washed me, and I returned the favor. We kissed and fondled each other intermittently.

After drying off, we moved towards my bed holding hands. My manhood gave away my expectations, and Laura giggled.

"I guess you have something in mind?"

"I have many things in mind."

We fell on the crisp clean sheets and kissed each other's face for a long time. It was all so natural, like we had done it a million times before.

"Laura, I have a drawer full of condoms."

"Don't worry about it. What are the odds?"

"Fine with me."

Our kissing spread to every conceivable part of our bodies. We teased and eased off numerous times. The sexual tension was wonderful.

I decided to take a more aggressive approach and give Laura what she needed most. I slid down between her legs. Every few seconds, the pace and intensity increased. Her body was responding beautifully, her breathing accelerated until she couldn't hold back any longer.

She grabbed my hair, shuddered uncontrollably and screamed out in total joy and ecstasy. I repeated this again and her orgasm arrived much sooner. Finally, we collapsed in each other's arms.

We hugged for a while, and she offered to return my favor. I declined indicating that this was her night. She was the star. I mounted her gently. She was very warm and receptive allowing me great access. Our body heat rose exponentially reflecting the increasing tempo of our bodies. When the moment arrived, we held each other tightly and screamed together.

After, Laura smiled at me and said, "You finally got what you always wanted."

"I sure did. Only it was even better than in my dreams."

"Your beautiful, and I love you. I've always loved you, my sweetheart." Laura smiled once again when she heard my words. It was so great to see this fabulous woman be so happy once again.

We fell asleep for an hour and made love again. I wanted to make up for lost time, and most importantly, I wanted Laura always at my side.

Epilogue

Damien was correct, I had no idea how large the porno business is in this country. When I brought W Pictures to market, the interest in the property was overwhelming. Surprisingly, Goldfarb's absence from the business ultimately increased the selling price of the company.

In the end, Donny Cohen's loan was repaid in full, including all fees and accrued interest. Too bad Donny was fired before this all happened. His boss, of course, took all the credit for resolving a very embarrassing situation for the bank and making some large profits.

More interestingly, Alan Goldfarb's net worth, already well into nine figures increased several hundred million more after the sale of W Pictures. As the sole owner of W, Goldfarb received all the proceeds after repayment of the bank loan.

Keep in mind, Alan was in jail serving a ten year sentence for raping Amanda Lane, so his net worth didn't do him much good presently.

Pyglet's reputation was saved by yours truly, the founder and CEO of the company. In fact, we earned all of the fees originally negotiated along with a very large bonus reflecting the successful sale of W Pictures.

Rob wasn't around to experience, first hand, the incredible M&A deal I orchestrated. Nor, would he share in the higher bonus pool resulting from the sale. I canned him the day after we had the conversation discussed earlier. He was really bitter, but I didn't care for two reasons. One, I paid him a ton of money over the years and also gave him a $2 million goodbye kiss. He had to agree not to compete with Pyglet for six months or steal any of my people.

Damien, after consulting with me, decided to apply to business school and will obtain an MBA. I thought this was an excellent career strategy given the difficult job market. Our relationship has been on the mend.

SS is still a vile bitch.

I attended the funeral of Alex Best. Very few people showed up to pay their respects. Very rude and inconsiderate. I guess she pissed off so many when she was alive, the offended just decided to boycott her last appearance. I was sad. I'm always sad at funerals.

Alex's murderers were never brought to justice, a final insult. The police were able to connect Alex to Jake Sardi. In fact, they believed she might have killed Jake, but dropped the case. Nobody really gave a shit about a punk.

Amanda Lane found closure when Goldfarb was convicted of raping her. He had the audacity to go to trial and testify that Amanda not only consented to sexual relations, but she seduced him. Given that Amanda was beaten up during his assault, I couldn't understand his legal strategy. Going to trial only served to increase the amount of time he was sentenced to by the judge.

In any case, Amanda went home to her parents. In a while, she expects to return to New York to resume her career.

Laura and I now are an item and plan to marry soon. You may ask, why the rush? Am I afraid of losing her? Actually no. She got pregnant the first time we made love. You may recall we left the condoms in the drawer and took the odds.

I'm very excited about my new life. I finally found the person I've been searching for. We get along great, and she helps me tremendously at Pyglet. I gave her Rob's office as an engagement gift along with a big diamond. Recently, she's been too fat to wear her white pants and thong.

www.ingramcontent.com/pod-product-compliance
Lightning Source LLC
Chambersburg PA
CBHW060242290526
45789CB00001B/161